THE JOY OF THRIVING
WHILE BLACK

THE JOY OF THRIVING WHILE BLACK

CHARISSE M. WILLIAMS

NEW DEGREE PRESS

THE JOY OF THRIVING WHILE BLACK

ISBN   978-1-63676-958-5   *Paperback*

           978-1-63730-024-4   *Kindle Ebook*

           978-1-63730-126-5   *Ebook*

*In memory of my mother, Willette Marie Sanders,
and my grandparents Wilhelmina Avery, Rufus
Sanders, Beatrice White, and Fred Williams.*

I am your wildest dreams.

CONTENTS

———

INTRODUCTION

———

"My mission in life is not merely to survive, but to thrive; and to do so with some passion, some compassion, some humor, and some style."

—MAYA ANGELOU

As a mother, divinity graduate student, and worker, Tricia Hersey was constantly exhausted. She decided to try an experiment: She took naps during the day wherever she could around campus. When all was said and done, she had found about ten sweet spots where she could nap.

Her experiment turned into an organization and a movement called the Nap Ministry. I heard Tricia Hersey talk about her work on the *Radiant Rest* podcast, and she shared this simple, powerful anecdote. Her grandmother, a mother of nine, migrated to Chicago from Mississippi to escape the terror of the Jim Crow South. Even though she had two jobs, "she sat on that couch for thirty minutes every day and rested her eyes."[1] Through her work with the Nap Ministry, Hersey is continuing this legacy of rest and self-care that can be so elusive for Black people.

This simple story captures the essence of this book. Part memoir, part invitation for self-reflection, *The Joy of Thriving While Black* is about the intersection of Blackness and well-being. There are so many barriers to thriving while Black in America, but somehow, many have done it. This book is an exploration of what makes this miracle possible.

The spark for *The Joy of Thriving While Black* was lit in the summer of 2020. In January, I launched my full-time leadership coaching practice. It was the second business I had started after a twenty-five-year career in nonprofit executive leadership. I was bright-eyed and hopeful, and the possibilities for my life and business felt endless. Then the coronavirus pandemic hit. Like so many business owners, I needed to figure out how to stay focused on my mission, pivot to work 100 percent virtually, and respond to the changing needs of my clients.

When I launched my coaching practice, all my one-on-one coaching clients were ambitious, high-performing executive leaders. I started out coaching on management and leadership issues. When the pandemic began, coaching conversations turned to managing stress and maintaining work/life balance. I fell in love with supporting my clients with those issues so much that I broadened my coaching practice to include leadership and well-being. *The Joy of Thriving While Black* is an extension of that work.

---

1   Tricia Hersey, "Rest–A Meticulous Love Practice with Tricia Hersey of The Nap Ministry," in *Radiant Rest Podcast with Tracee Stanley,* produced by Baron Rinzler, podcast, 24:03.

WHILE BLACK

There is an old saying that when white America catches a cold, Black America catches pneumonia. The impact of the coronavirus pandemic was a painful example of that. Black folks experienced a disproportionate number of hospitalizations and deaths due to underlying health issues, inadequate access to medical care, and the racism that plagues the medical system. The economic impact of the pandemic also affected Black folks the most, with job losses hitting the lowest-paid jobs the hardest.

The economic forecasts freaked me out. I had sold my house the year before and was living with my cousin Kanika in the suburbs of Atlanta. It was an incredible blessing. It allowed me to save money while I built my business and enjoy some precious family time. I was fortunate to have savings, but as a new business owner, it was humbling to be working my tail off while watching my bank balance decrease month after month. I was worried about how the pandemic would affect the viability of my business and earning trajectory.

Then came the summer of 2020, which was unlike anything I had experienced in my lifetime. By then, Ahmaud Arbery, Breonna Taylor, George Floyd, and Rayshard Brooks had been killed by police and wannabe police.[2] The video footage of three of the killings was on a continuous loop. I was living in Georgia, right outside of Atlanta. People had been protesting for a couple of weeks straight, and the city of Atlanta was under curfew. Working, processing the news, and digesting all the social media posts flooding my feeds was mentally and emotionally exhausting.

---

2   Khaleda Rahman, "From George Floyd to Breonna Taylor, Remembering the Black People Killed by Police in 2020," *Newsweek*, December 29, 2020.

While violence against Black Americans is as old as America itself, something about the summer of 2020 was different. This came to be known as a racial mega-threat, "a negative, large-scale, race-related event that receives significant media attention—which heightens racial trauma. Research shows that this type of ongoing experience creates psychological, racial battle fatigue."[3] Every person I talked to was talking about the killings. That, combined with the pandemic and economic forecasts, created a triple layer of stress, fear, and uncertainty, and I was feeling it.

The killings reflected the systemic racism built into the very fabric of America, beginning with the genocide of Native American peoples and the transatlantic slave trade. The culture, policy, practices, and laws that govern the United States of America were designed to create barriers to thriving while Black. In his seminal essay, *The Case for Reparations*, Ta-Nehisi Coates begins with:

"Two hundred fifty years of slavery. Ninety years of Jim Crow. Sixty years of separate but equal. Thirty-five years of racist housing policy. Until we reckon with our compounding moral debts, America will never be whole."[4]

Everything felt broken.

SPARKED BY JOY

On June 7, 2020, I had just finished working out, and I was sitting in a rocking chair on the front porch soaking up the

---

3   Danielle D. King, Abdifatah A. Ali, Courtney L. McCluney, and Courtney Bryant, "Give Black Employees Time to Rest and Recover," *Harvard Business Review*, February 22, 2021.

4   Ta-Nehisi Coates, "The Case for Reparations," *The Atlantic*, June 2014.

sun. I was experiencing a moment of peace and grace. While scrolling through my social media feed, I noticed the hashtag "#blackjoymatters." Then I found "#blackjoyisresistance" and "#blackjoyisrevolutionary." I spent the next hour voraciously consuming as much uplifting content about Black folks as possible. I needed to be reminded that there was still so much joy, even for Black folks in 2020. The more I looked, the more I found.

As I continued to explore, I started asking myself how I could use my work, my voice, my coaching, and life experiences to contribute to the conversation about racial justice and the well-being of Black folks. By the summer of 2020, I had been sheltering in place because of the pandemic for four months, with no end in sight. I decided that the book I thought I would write "one day" should be written now. That is how *The Joy of Thriving While Black* was born.

The title "*The Joy of Thriving While Black*" is a play on and an antidote to all the things that racism makes harder for Black people, sometimes even costing us our lives. That list includes jogging, holding a cellphone, sleeping, bird watching, holding Arizona iced tea and Skittles, and finally, so common that it has its own acronym, Driving While Black (DWB). This idea is captured in a beautiful, chilling poem by my friend Derrick Weston Brown, whose refrain is "We Can't Have Nothing."[5] Derrick wrote the poem in 2015 in response to a white gunman killing nine Black people in a church in Charleston, South Carolina.[6] Sadly, the poem could have been written in 2020, 1920 or 1820.

---

5   Derrick Weston Brown, "We Can't Have Nothing," AJ+, July 15, 2020, YouTube video, 3:22.

6   Samuel Momodu, "The Charleston Church Massacre (2015)," *BlackPast. org*, September 30, 2017.

Once the idea for *The Joy of Thriving While Black* grabbed me, it would not let me go. When I started, I didn't know this project would become one of my self-care rituals. Whenever I was having a hard day, feeling discouraged, isolated, or weary, I would have another interview for *The Joy of Thriving While Black*. Every single conversation left me with more energy, hope, and feeling connected to the person I interviewed. The entire process was affirming and healing.

THRIVING DEFINED

As a leadership coach, I've spent a good deal of time studying, thinking about, teaching, and coaching on what it takes to thrive. A lot has been written on the subject. One of the most cited scholars is Abraham Maslow. He proposed a hierarchy of needs in his 1943 paper, "A Theory of Human Motivation."[7] Those needs, which can be visualized like a pyramid, include basic survival needs like food, sleep, and water on the bottom. Self-actualization and fulfillment are on the top. Maslow's critics found these needs to be too limiting and linear. His theory seemed to suggest that someone who was very poor, for example, could not have a profound sense of purpose.

One of Maslow's critics was Manfred Max-Neef. His research led him to define a broader range of human needs, including the need for rest, creativity, and freedom.[8] This theory would explain why people, since the beginning of time, even when living from hunt to hunt, harvest to harvest, still adorn themselves, dance, and make art and music.

---

7   Saul McCleod, "Maslow's Hierarchy of Needs," *Simple Psychology,* December 29, 2020.

8   "Needs," Environmental Justice Organisations, Liabilities and Trade, accessed February 26, 2021.

All of this scholarship planted the seeds for the field of positive psychology as it is known today. For decades, psychologists were concerned with diagnosing and fixing what made people suffer. Positive psychology takes the opposite approach. It is a research-based, scientific approach "to studying human thoughts, feelings, and behavior, with a focus on strengths instead of weaknesses, building the good in life instead of repairing the bad."[9] Out of positive psychology came Martin Seligman's influential PERMA model of well-being. The "P" is for positive emotion, "E" is for engagement, "R" is for relationships, "M" is for meaning, and "A" is for accomplishment and achievement.[10] This helped further codify the ingredients of a life well lived.

Over the years, the study of happiness and human flourishing has exploded. Some studies, including Dan Buettner's "Blue Zones," explore what makes groups of people in entire regions live long and thrive.[11] As a coach and student of positive psychology, I find these models helpful for understanding what it means to thrive. But here is what's discouraging: I have yet to come across research that identifies places where Black folks are thriving. While it's disappointing, it's not surprising. *What* you find depends upon *where* you're looking and *who* is doing the looking.

My definition of thriving is to have what you need internally and externally to grow, flourish, and make your highest contribution as a human being while also enjoying the

---

9   Courtney E. Ackerman, "What Is Positive Psychology & Why Is It Important?" *PositivePsychology.com*, June 12, 2020.

10   Ibid.

11   "Original Blue Zones Explorations," Blue Zones, accessed February 26, 2021.

joys and pleasures of life. I believe all human beings need the same things to thrive. However, thriving in the face of systemic racism and other threats to Black lives means Black people need additional spaces to come together for collective comfort, care, and refuge.

Writing *The Joy of Thriving While Black* allowed me to excavate my memories and share what I have learned about thriving. It also gave me the opportunity to explore the stories of other Black folks who had insights into what it takes to thrive and how they help others do the same. *The Joy of Thriving While Black* is not a research study, nor is it a formula for happiness. It is part memoir, part invitation for self-reflection, providing stories and anecdotes from my personal experience and my interviewees.

As I mined my experience and those of the people I interviewed, it became very clear that thriving while Black is both an individual pursuit and a collective experience. We enable our ability to thrive by adopting habits and mindsets like self-care, rest, and resilience. The collective experience of thriving includes lifting others up through activism, community building, and creating safe spaces.

When I first started this book, I made a long list of people I wanted to interview. In the process, I was reminded that I know some really amazing human beings. They are authors, entrepreneurs and CEOs, artists, poets, and activists. Many are family members and friends. It is my honor to share their stories.

THEMES

The Joy of Thriving While Black is organized into three parts and covers ten themes related to the actions, mindsets, and conditions conducive to thriving while Black.

PART I - "WHEN I DARE TO BE POWERFUL, TO USE MY STRENGTH IN THE SERVICE OF MY VISION, THEN IT BECOMES LESS AND LESS IMPORTANT WHETHER I AM AFRAID." —AUDRE LORDE

Part one is about vision and includes chapters on **purpose, activism,** and **pride.**

One story featured in the chapter on activism is about Oronike Odeleye. Oronike grew up in Atlanta in a family that viewed political action as a critical tool for improving the community and the country. A fierce advocate of young women and girls, she started hearing rumors of a very popular musician abusing girls with impunity. This was happening right in her backyard of Atlanta. What she did about it sparked a national conversation about the sexual exploitation of Black girls. In collaboration with other leaders, her work eventually grew into a powerful movement.

PART II - "IF YOU WANT TO GO FAST, GO ALONE; IF YOU WANT TO GO FAR, GO TOGETHER." —AFRICAN PROVERB

Part two examines the collective nature of thriving and contains chapters on **community, safe spaces,** and **family.**

In the chapter on safe spaces, I examine the need for spaces for people of color to learn, grow, and support one another in ways that can be challenging in majority-white spaces. I share the inspiring story of author and yoga teacher Octavia Raheem. She created Starshine & Clay, a yoga and meditation community dedicated to the transformation, well-being, and care of Black women and women of color. It is a sacred, beautiful space to which I am grateful to belong.

**PART III - "I THOUGHT I TOLD YOU THAT WE WON'T STOP" —
MULTIPLE ARTISTS**

The final section of the book is about habits and mindsets that
contribute to well-being and thriving, including **resilience,
self-care, rest,** and **joy.**

Jasán Ward epitomizes joy. Life has thrown many health
challenges his way, but he bounces back time and again, fill-
ing the world with dance, poetry, and laughter. Along the way,
he has had a positive impact on many people's lives.

Every chapter ends with questions to help you explore
what each theme means to you. The final chapter, Putting It
into Practice, coaches you through exercises to help you take
actions to thrive more.

The Joy of Thriving While Black was written with a Black
reader in mind. Some questions at the end of the chapters
reference the reader's Blackness specifically, like, "When did
you first learn what it meant to be 'Black'? How did you feel?"
These questions, however, translate across a diverse set of
identities and life experiences.

**Here are my biggest dreams for *The Joy of Thriving
While Black*:**

- I hope you will *feel* inspired by the stories, your humanity
  affirmed in the process.
- I hope you will *explore* and *discover* what makes you
  thrive while learning some basic research and science
  around thriving, happiness, and flourishing.
- I hope you will *believe,* with all your heart, that through
  your mindset and the support of community, you
  can thrive.
- I hope you will be *motivated* and then *take action* to
  cultivate conditions to help you thrive more.

I give you *The Joy of Thriving While Black* with a heart bursting with love and gratitude. It is a prayer, a hope, and an offering to remind us of who we are and have always been. We survive. We rise. We thrive with passion, compassion, humor, and style.

PART I

"When I dare to be powerful, to use my strength in the service of my vision, then it becomes less and less important whether I am afraid."

—AUDRE LORDE

CHAPTER 1

PURPOSE

"You would rather find purpose than a job or career. It is the reason you are on the planet at this particular time in history. Whatever you choose to do, remember the struggles along the way are only meant to shape you for your purpose."

—CHADWICK BOSEMAN

I was giddy, nervous, and, at times, downright terrified. I had left a very good, mid-six-figure job with benefits, generous leave, and amazing colleagues. I was starting over and channeling all my life experience and skills into a new leadership coaching business. I was betting on myself, ready to fully embrace my purpose.

A couple of weeks before my business launch, I went to Starshine & Clay, a weekend retreat for women of color created by author, mentor, and yoga teacher Octavia Raheem. On Sunday, January 12, 2020, the final morning of the retreat, I sat on my meditation cushion facing east and bathed in the light of the rising sun. It had been a long time since I meditated with my eyes open, and the view from the top of the mountain in Sautee Nacoochee, Georgia, was stunning. I sat, breathing steadily and deeply, trying to be present as my mind wandered to all that had happened over the weekend and all the challenges that lied ahead. I also thought of everyone who came before me, including my ancestors and the indigenous peoples for whom the village of Sautee Nacoochee was named.

I was sitting on hallowed ground surrounded by forty other women. The retreat theme, "Facing the Rising Sun," was inspired by James Weldon Johnson's poem that became the anthem "Lift Every Voice and Sing."[12] As we were finishing our meditation, our resident retreat serenader, Malesha Taylor, began humming the anthem. With no explicit instruction, we all began humming along until we were eventually standing, holding hands, and belting out the song with all of our hearts and souls.

I drove home from the retreat feeling relaxed and rested. I was ready to engage in the final preparations for my business launch party.

A lawyer by training, I had worked in the nonprofit and social justice sectors for twenty-five years at organizations focused on human rights, education, and criminal and juvenile justice reform. I was proud of the fact that all my work had a measurable, positive impact on the world. I felt ready to have a different impact.

My path to becoming a full-time leadership coach was inspired by professional coaches who supported me

---

12 "NAACP History: Lift Every Voice and Sing," NAACP, accessed January 14, 2021.

throughout my career. They were thought partners and strategists who, through artful questioning, helped me make progress toward my goals. They helped me see myself more clearly by repeating what they heard me say and making thoughtful observations about whether my habits and mindsets were helping me or hindering me. I wanted to do for others what they did for me.

Having been a consultant previously, I loved the idea that in coaching, the client is the expert, and the coach is there to offer support. So, in 2019, I decided to complete a coaching certification with JRNI or "journey" Life Coaching and loved it so much that after I graduated, I became an instructor for the program.

My personal health and wellness journey also led me to become a certified yoga teacher. That began a new chapter in my quest to become a more mindful leader on and off the yoga mat. In previous jobs, I was constantly seeking more work/life balance, but I wanted something even better—alignment. I wanted everything I did personally and professionally to be aligned with my values, gifts, and purpose. Coaching was the vehicle for doing that.

One thing I loved about my training and work as a leadership coach was that it provided me great insight into what makes people thrive or flourish. A study published in the *Journal of the American Medical Association* found that a strong sense of purpose is associated with decreased mortality and other health benefits. The article defines purpose as the integration of *"who you are* with *what you do."*[13]

---

13 Scott Mautz, "A 27-Year Study Says 1 Thing Is Key to Happiness and Longevity in Work and Life," *Inc.*, August 14, 2019.

My definition of purpose can be captured in this formula: who you are + what you are good at *and* love to do + what the world needs + how you want to feel. Here is mine: *I am an author, coach, and speaker. My purpose is to live a joyful, connected, and prosperous life and to use my talents, strengths, and life experiences to help others do the same.*

THE BIG LAUNCH

After seven months of planning, January 22, 2020 finally arrived—the day of my business launch party. I had tossed around several different locations for the party but landed on my parents' house in Smyrna, right outside of Atlanta. I wanted the event to be warm and intimate, and it was.

I held the launch party in their living room, which was a warm mustard yellow and flanked on one side by floor-to-ceiling bookshelves. They contained books, family photos, and other mementos. The focal point was a large, red, L-shaped leather sofa with a marble coffee table in the front. The room was an open concept with an adjacent kitchen and an island in the center. The food and drinks were plentiful and included salmon, roasted veggies, and miniature desserts. The entire scene was a visual feast.

Until that day, I had been excited and a bundle of nerves. *Had I spent too much money on everything or not enough? Who was coming, who was not, and would I have enough food? Would people "get" what I was doing with my new business?*

After all, I was leaving behind titles and organizations that conferred status, were easily understood, and well respected. Coaching was an emerging field with many amazing, caring professionals but also a fair share of folks with great marketing skills who consistently overpromised and under-delivered. The latter gives our profession a bad name.

When it came time to speak, my doubts faded into the background. I first took a deep breath and scanned the room. Gazing up at me were clients, those I wanted to court, and former students. Some of my Leadership Atlanta classmates were there, along with family and close girlfriends. As I took the breath that would carry me through my opening words, I was filled with gratitude. None of my doubts and fears mattered anymore. Everyone who needed to be there was present, and I was ready to share my story. My life and career had been anything but linear, but everything I had experienced up to that point had prepared me for that moment to lean into my purpose and shout it to the rooftops.

I thanked everyone and told them my plans for my business and how they could support me. Looking back on my closing remarks, they seem prophetic:

"I want to close with this: I am here to boldly tell you that I plan to have the most wildly successful coaching practice imaginable. The work I have described to you is just the beginning. I've been writing a lot and see books in my future. I also envision online classes and massive events. I am just really happy to have you all here at the beginning."

The program ended with Malesha Taylor singing "*O mio bab-bino caro*" by Giacomo Puccini.[14] I had met Malesha for the first time at the Starshine & Clay retreat earlier that month. The moment I heard her voice, I knew I wanted her to sing at my event. The plan was for her to begin with the song

---

14   "What are the lyrics and translation of 'O mio babbino caro'?" Classic FM, accessed March 14, 2021.

by Puccini, then sing "Golden" by Jill Scott, and we would all sing along. But after she finished "*O mio babbino caro,*" I knew that the proverbial microphone had been dropped. Nothing more needed to be sung or said. I was in a living room with people who loved and supported me. I had shared my vision for my business, which was an extension of my purpose. I was ready to begin.

I was excited to explore how other Black folks found their purpose and how it contributed to their ability to thrive.

WHAT ARE WE GOING TO DO?

What do President Joseph Biden, Vice President Kamala Harris, Stacey Abrams, and Senators Raphael Warnock and Jon Ossoff have in common? They all leveraged the space, leadership, and community at The Gathering Spot (TGS) in Atlanta to build their campaigns and movements.

The first time I visited TGS was in 2016 during the Many Rivers to Cross Social Justice, Music, and Arts Festival. The festival was organized by Sankofa, singer and activist Harry Belafonte's social justice organization. They hosted a panel discussion with Mr. Belafonte and several local artists and activists at TGS. I had been hearing a lot about TGS and was excited to check it out. That's how I met Ryan Wilson, cofounder and CEO.

Ryan's accomplishments belie his thirty years. He and his work have been featured in *Inc., Forbes,* and *Fast Company.* He has won numerous awards, and he is a sought-after speaker about all things tech and entrepreneurship. When I asked Ryan, "What does it mean to you to thrive?" he responded, "Really living your purpose, being fulfilled with where things are in your life, and hopefully making a meaningful contribution to whatever you're most passionate about."

Ryan had been interested in diversity, inclusion, and politics for as long as he could remember. Watching political talk shows with his family as a child was a highlight of his week. An Atlanta native, Ryan could see himself and his family in every passage of Dr. King's "I Have a Dream" speech. He always felt that his purpose was to engage in topics related to justice and equality, to carry on the tradition handed down to him. Growing up in relative privilege with parents who were successful entrepreneurs, Ryan always had access to both white and Black America. He believed that access gave him certain responsibilities. Though he has always been exposed to social justice leaders, his personal call to service came into focus when he was an undergraduate student at Georgetown University.

At Georgetown, Ryan was one of the Student Commission for Unity leaders charged with analyzing the university's diversity and inclusion efforts. The group ended up writing a 350-page research report and recommendations. The president of the university accepted the recommendations, which became a catalyst for change. Following the report's acceptance, Ryan worked with the dean of admissions and the vice president of the university to create a plan of action. The experience was formative because he saw the power of having an idea that you're passionate about and being able to make a change, even at a powerful institution like Georgetown.

The seed for TGS was planted in 2013 after Trayvon Martin, a seventeen-year-old African American high school student, was fatally shot while walking home from a convenience store. His killer, George Zimmerman, had been following Trayvon around the neighborhood and claimed he was armed and dangerous. He was armed alright—with a pack of Skittles and a bottle of Arizona Iced Tea.[15]

Ryan and his friends were emailing back and forth about the incident when someone sent a question that would change the course of Ryan's life and career: "What are we going to do?" Ryan responded, "Wouldn't it be cool to have a club in DC that would be used for people to come together and discuss, then act on ideas? A cross between a think tank and a country club, minus the elitism." He then imagined this being "a place where thinkers, activists, business folks, politicians, and most importantly, the average person, could go to discuss ideas and social issues."[16]

After Ryan graduated from Georgetown's undergraduate and law schools, he went to work at a law firm in Atlanta. But the question posed in the email exchanged between him and his friends continued to pull at him. His response crystalized a new way for him to manifest his purpose.

In 2016, he and his friend and fellow Georgetown student, T.K. Petersen, founded TGS. Its mission is "to create a world where opportunity is the byproduct of community and collaboration."[17] By 2021, it had over 2,500 members between Atlanta and its newest location in Washington, DC. The members are predominantly African American, ranging from ages twenty-one to eighty-eight years old. The eldest member is Ambassador Andrew Young.

I deeply admire Ryan. He was in his mid-twenties when the idea for TGS took root. He harnessed his community and

---

15 Greg Botelho, "What Happened the Night Trayvon Martin Died," *CNN*, May 23, 2012.

16 *This Is Why We Gather* (Atlanta: The Gathering Spot Holdings, LLC, 2020), 10

17 "Mission," The Gathering Spot, accessed January 14, 2021.

resources, followed through, and executed until his vision became a reality. His approach to his work is passionate, purposeful, and unapologetically Black.

In February 2021, Ryan and T.K. were invited to speak to Nike's Global Black Employee Network. Ryan addressed the common question about whether creating something that targets Black people is too niche. He responded, "Everybody is trying to access what we do and what we create as Black people. What we're tapping into, it's not niche. I refuse to talk about it like it's a small thing because it is a big thing."[18]

By following his purpose and creating TGS, Ryan Wilson is helping so many people, including me, find support for their purpose and dreams. It is a really big thing.

In chapter four, Community, I revisit the role that TGS has played in my life.

GUIDED BY THE ANCESTORS

The process of seeking out more stories about purpose led me to reconnect with a dear friend, Ifé Milligan. We met in 2002 in an Afro-Cuban dance class in Washington, DC. Time, my move to Atlanta, and her move to Virginia Beach put distance between us, but we found we were still on parallel paths.

While she would not have called it "purpose" at the time, Ifé Milligan developed a strong sense of what she wanted to do with her life when she was sixteen years old. In a high school psychology class, she learned about the brain and the way people suffered when they were mentally ill. She knew she wanted to help in some way.

---

18   Ryan Wilson, "As we close out Black History Month let's not forget that there isn't anything small or niche about Black people or Black culture," LinkedIn, February 27, 2021.

Ifé was raised in St. Croix, Virgin Islands, in a family of spiritual people with unique gifts of "seeing, hearing, and feeling things." The woman with the most extraordinary gifts in this department was her paternal great-grandmother, Christiana "Shana" Sackey. Granny Sackey maintained an altar with candles and glasses of water on top, and she prayed with the rosary she always carried around. Granny Sackey was also a healer who set bones and made tinctures and teas to help people with various ailments. She used to pray at the crossroads whenever there was a problem. In African and African American cosmology, the crossroads is the place where decisions are made. It is a physical representation of the supplicant's intentions.

Granny Sackey had sixteen children. When Ifé's father, Sakey's grandson, was thirteen, he went to live with her. They had a very special, close relationship. Although Granny Sackey died the year before Ifé was born, Ifé feels a special connection to her. She is one of Ife's spiritual guides. According to Ifé, "The more I acknowledge Shana's presence, the more that I acknowledge my own spiritual gifts and the more I attract what I want."

After high school, Ifé earned her bachelor's degree in psychology and a master's in clinical social work. After ten years of doing one-on-one therapy, she started to feel burnt out, so she went on to work in managed health care. She worked at a corporation as a behavioral health manager, where she managed a team of clinicians in various psychiatric facilities. The company was expanding, and Ifé had the most prestigious job she had ever held and was making the most money ever. There was only one problem: Ifé became profoundly unhappy and unfulfilled. She explained, "I was doing a job that was so far away from my purpose, and every day I went to work, I felt more and more insecure about my purpose and my gifts."

In 2008, Ifé had been initiated as a priest in the Orisha tradition. It is a spiritual path that originated with the Yoruba people of Nigeria and spread across the Americas as a result of the trans-Atlantic slave trade. The Orishas are spiritual powers related to forces of nature and aspects of the human character. Because the practice of African religions was outlawed during slavery, devotees disguised their practices by syncretizing Orishas with Catholic saints.[19] By practicing African-centered spirituality, Ifé was following in her great grandmother Shana's footsteps.

After becoming a priest, Ifé started taking on godchildren and guiding them along their spiritual paths. She loved this work but hated that she had to squeeze it between meetings, lunch breaks, and after work. She was living two different lives, and it just wasn't working.

Ifé took a step back to heed the ancestral guidance that grounded her spiritually:

"There are so many outside influences that create a lot of anxiety, confusion, insecurity, doubt and fear. Some of that is internal until we get to a place where we finally surrender. And we stop fighting. I took my hands off the wheel and I completely surrendered to spirit."

When Ifé surrendered, she went through what she describes as the midlife awakening that guided her closer to her purpose.

---

19 "Sacred Arts of Orisha Traditions," Georgetown University Library, accessed February 28, 2021.

By the time she had been working for her company for nine years, she had a premonition that a major change was coming. Something told her, "Save your money, Ifé; save your money." The day after her last annual review, which was stellar as always, Ifé's boss told her they needed to have a chat. Her position was being eliminated. At first, she panicked, but as the news sunk in, she thought to herself, *I'm free, I'm free.*

Ifé didn't know exactly what her next chapter would look like, but she knew she wanted to serve people combining her mental health background and role as a spiritual advisor. She spent the next six months preparing. In order to expand her skill set beyond her master's in social work, she decided to pursue her coaching certification. She wasn't sure where it fit into the grand scheme, but she just went with it. "Living in her purpose," as she described it, allowed her to trust the process and be at peace, even though she faced a lot of uncertainty.

After her six-month sabbatical, she went back to work as a therapist, but on a part-time basis. That gave her more time to be a spiritual guide and lead women's empowerment groups. She had so much more confidence because of her age and life experience, which allowed her to be herself completely. "When I started believing more in myself, that's when I noticed some shifts in terms of the amount of work that I attracted and the opportunities. The little miracles and all these things started happening because I was finally in a place where I was okay saying, *You know what? I'm pretty dope.*"

Ifé told me that she is in the midst of her mid-life "awakening." In our conversation, our first in many years, we noticed many parallels in our paths. I have found my professional passion and purpose through combining two decades of nonprofit leadership experience with yoga, meditation, and coaching. It's not the kind of career laid out for you in elementary school. Ifé could relate, and she shared, "I too am in a place where I feel like I am finally thriving. I am not making as much money as I used to make, but I am the most content and the most at peace that I've been in my whole life, finally at almost forty-nine."

Purpose is not only what you choose to do but also how you show up in every aspect of your life. I deeply believe that we all have a purpose—a reason for being here right now. We owe it to ourselves and the world to explore it and express it in the best way we can.

Sometimes people get nervous about investigating their purpose. They are afraid it means they have to find a new job or start a business. That was my path and Ryan's path, but it's not necessary. Clarifying her purpose actually brought Ifé back to her work as a therapist, with greater confidence.

In this and the following chapters, I invite you to explore the questions at the end. You can journal your thoughts or talk about them with a friend. You can also just read a question, sit still and quiet, and see what arises. If you are aching for clarity about your purpose, these questions are a good place to start.

QUESTIONS FOR EXPLORATION

1. How do you define your purpose in life? If that question feels too big, explore this formula: Who you are + what you are good at *and* love to do + what the world needs + how you want to feel.
2. How does your sense of purpose impact your day-to-day activities and decisions?
3. Who do you admire for their strong sense of purpose?

4. One of Maya Angelou's most famous quotes is, "I've learned that people will forget what you said, people will forget what you did, but people will never forget how you made them feel." How do you want to make people feel?
5. Who can support you in living your most purpose-filled life?

CHAPTER 2

ACTIVISM

———

"I'm no longer accepting the things I cannot change...I'm changing the things I cannot accept."

—ANGELA DAVIS

The year was 1969. A strange, warm light came from outside the window of Wari House, a cooperative residence for Black women students at Cornell University. The light quickly grew bright enough to wake up the residents. The young women who lived in the building ran outside at 3 a.m. to see a flaming cross in their yard. The next morning, in protest, members of the Afro-American Society staged a takeover of Willard Straight Hall, a prominent building where students gathered.[20] Entering as an undergraduate student at Cornell in 1989, I felt their activism and its legacy as a palpable presence on campus. It inspired me to find my own way throughout my life to change the things that I could not accept.

---

20 George Lowery, "A Campus Takeover That Symbolized an Era of Change," *Cornell Chronicle*, April 16, 2009.

The Black student takeover of Willard Straight Hall was a response to the overwhelmingly Eurocentric curriculum and the poor treatment of Black students. The students remained in the building for thirty-five hours negotiating with the administration. The takeover resulted in a seven-point agreement that included establishing the Africana Studies and Research Center and Ujamaa Residential College.[21] Twenty years later, I was a direct beneficiary of their protest and activism. I entered Cornell as an Africana Studies major and lived in Ujamaa (Swahili for "family") during my freshman year.

One professor who had a profound impact on me was Dr. James Turner. Professor Turner created Cornell's Black Studies program and coined the term "Africana."[22] He was recruited to Cornell following the 1969 student protest. I took two classes with him filled with equal parts fear and awe. He was infamous for his intense Socratic questioning and for calling on students when they did not have their hands raised. If you were prepared, you had the opportunity to discuss and banter with one of the most brilliant minds I have ever encountered. He was quick-witted and sometimes downright playful.

If you weren't prepared? Oh, Lawd! Dr. Turner would make you question your very existence. While I never heard him say these exact words, his lectures delivered to you personally, in front of the entire class, boiled down to this: "How dare you have the privilege of being a Black student at Cornell studying Africana Studies and show up in class unprepared?

---

21   "History of Africana Studies at Cornell," Cornell University, accessed January 29, 2021.

22   Yvette Lisa Ndlovu, "Africana Center to Honor Founder at 50th Anniversary Symposium." *Cornell Chronicle*, April 9, 2019.

How dare you disgrace the struggles that led you here? Cornell was founded when our ancestors were still enslaved! Do you not remember the Willard Straight Hall takeover?"

Cornell University sits on 2,300 acres of rolling hills in Ithaca, New York, and the Africana Studies and Research center was on the far edge of campus, straight uphill. If you were late to class and complained about the hike, this could be part memory, part myth, but Dr. Turner might just remind you of how far Harriet Tubman walked to free enslaved people.

Dr. Turner put in me the fear of God and the inspiration of my ancestors. I got involved in every student protest I could on issues ranging from financial aid cuts to threats to campus programs that supported students of color. I remember participating in a student takeover of Day Hall, which housed the financial aid office. We sat surrounding the building, chanting late into the night. Some of our professors, including Dr. Turner, visited us to offer support and words of encouragement. He was also very clear that we had to "study and struggle." That meant he expected us to be in class the next day, on time, having done the reading.

That mantra "study and struggle" stayed with me. I wasn't sure how I wanted to apply it to the world of work, but it became a part of my core value system. After undergraduate school, I did what any bright young person with a liberal arts degree does who wants to make a difference in the world—I applied for nonprofit jobs.

My first job was at YouthVision, a youth development organization that worked to create more opportunities for young people to grow into thriving adults. At the time, in the mid-nineties, our work was being undermined by increasingly regressive juvenile justice legislation. In my opinion,

Illinois—the state with the first juvenile court—had become the "try kids as adults, lock them up, and throw away the key" state.[23] To learn more about juvenile justice policy, I took a fateful trip to Northwestern University's Children and Family Justice Center. There I met Bernardine Dohrn and Cheryl Graves, renowned juvenile justice advocates and two of my heroines to this day.

That day, I learned about how many kids were in pretrial detention in the overcrowded Cook County Juvenile Detention Center. Legally, they were supposed to be adjudicated as "delinquent" and moved to another detention center or released within thirty days. Instead, many were languishing in detention for more than two years, not having been convicted of anything. These kids were overwhelmingly Black and Brown. I decided to go to law school so I could free the children.

I attended Northwestern Law School and volunteered for a weekly program at the detention center called "Girl Talk." We did art, creative writing, dance, theater, and all kinds of cool programs with the girls. We even got clearance to create a rooftop garden. One week, I brought in my yoga teacher, Yirser Ra Hotep, to do yoga with the girls. I will never forget one girl telling us after class that it was the first time she had ever felt peaceful. It was fun, rewarding work, but also heartbreaking.

The dark, windowless space smelled perpetually of body odor. Many of the guards were rude and seemed to instigate conflict more than trying to maintain calm. I eventually learned they earned very low pay and required little

---

23 "Juvenile Justice History," Center on Juvenile and Criminal Justice, accessed January 29, 2021.

specialized education to do their demanding, complex, and sometimes dangerous jobs. The staff was overwhelmingly Black. They were, in effect, locked up too.

I graduated from Northwestern and passed the bar exam but didn't become a juvenile defense attorney. My eyes had been opened to the inequities of the juvenile and criminal justice systems, and I would continue to work to change the system in any way that I could. I landed a job as the program officer for the juvenile and criminal justice programs at the Public Welfare Foundation in Washington, DC. At the Foundation, I facilitated the financial support of incredible organizations around the country like the Southern Center for Human Rights, Families against Mandatory Minimums, and The Innocence Project New Orleans. Because of my work at the Public Welfare Foundation, I got to meet one of my personal heroes, Bryan Stevenson—lawyer, advocate, and founder of Equal Justice Initiative of Alabama.

I stand on the shoulders of Dr. James Turner and so many others who commit to changing the things they can no longer accept. Those changes don't have to be monumental. As politician and activist Stacey Abrams shared in a 2021 article:

"I've always wanted to leave breadcrumbs—like my mentor, Miss Cicely Tyson, did for me—and leave the world a little shifted by my presence. Not everyone can be a Martin Luther King Jr., but they can be who they are and make a difference in the life of someone."[24]

---

24 Angelique Jackson and Jazz Tangcay, "Viola Davis and Stacey Abrams on Oscar Season, Politics and Wielding Their Power as Black Women," Variety, February 17, 2021.

Our methods may range from protesting, to writing, to providing legal representation or social services. It's just important to do something to make it easier for Black folks to thrive as a collective.

WHILE BLACK

It was a rainy day in January 2008, soon after Barack Obama's presidential inauguration. Hillary Dunson was among the scores of people who were overcome with joy about what Obama's election meant to the country. She was moving through life with more hope for the country's future than she'd had for a while.

Needing to take her ten-year-old daughter Haley to the orthodontist, she picked her up from school in Midtown Atlanta to drive her to the appointment. As she was exiting the highway and approaching a red light, Hillary's foot slipped off the pedal, and she rear-ended the truck in front of her. The other driver had one of those enormous pickup trucks with a ball on the back for hitching a load. His truck wasn't damaged at all, but the grill was cracked on Hillary's Range Rover Sport. When the other driver got out of the car, he said, "Ooh, it looks like that might be pretty expensive to fix. You should probably get a police report to help you with the insurance process." Hillary thought that made sense, so she called the police.

When the police arrived, they checked her ID and the other driver's, asked him a couple of questions, and then let him go. The responding officer returned to his vehicle with her license, and soon another officer arrived, which surprised Hillary. Both officers approached her, told her that she had an outstanding ticket, and that her license was suspended. She knew for certain that she had paid her last ticket and didn't have a suspended license. She communicated that to the officers. One of them said, "Ma'am, we're going to need to take you down to the station to sort this out." Up to that point, their exchange had been civil. When she questioned why she needed to go to the station, referencing the presence of her young daughter, the atmosphere became more tense.

Hillary could feel the panic rising in her chest as the reality sank in that they were intent on taking her away. With part anger and part fear, she asked what she was supposed to do with her daughter. The officer said that Hillary needed to call someone to get her. Because her husband was relatively far away, with trembling hands, Hillary began phoning friends who lived nearby. When she didn't reach anyone, she called her husband, who immediately dropped his work on one of his dental patients, saying, "I'm on my way!"

No less than ten minutes later, the officers were getting impatient, telling her that her husband was taking too long. At that point, their tone was hostile. "I'm sorry, ma'am, we've waited long enough. We need to take you in now."

Hillary was trying to hold it together but was on the verge of tears. "What am I supposed to do with my daughter?"

They told her that one of the officers would stay with her. Hillary replied, "I don't know you; I'm not leaving my daughter with you!" She was still somewhat in shock that this was even happening but understood that she needed to remain calm or things would continue to escalate.

Hillary called her husband, who was en route, explained the situation, and gave the phone to her daughter Haley. She told her, "Daddy's on the line. No matter what happens, do not hang up this phone. Stay on the phone until he gets here. Sit in the car with the doors locked and do not open them for any reason." She then handed Haley her personal items, including her purse, and turned to go with the police.

"Ma'am, we're going to have to cuff you." Again, Hillary protested, asking why that was necessary when she was going willingly.

"It's protocol, ma'am. But we can do it on the other side of the squad car, so your daughter doesn't see it."

Haley saw everything.

When Hillary arrived at the station, she was pushed and pulled around like she wasn't human. She undressed in front of a guard, was given a rough uniform and dirty slides to wear on her feet. She sat in a cell with seven or eight other women, including one who was pregnant. A toilet in the room shielded the user with a partial wall, but it did not have the privacy of a regular bathroom.

Because it was after banking hours, Hillary's husband had to call friends and neighbors to round up the $1,500 cash needed to bail her out.

When Hillary was released, she was so angry. She knew things like this happened but never thought it would happen to her. Her nice clothes and car, education, and relative privilege could not shield her from the dangers of driving while Black. She hadn't done anything wrong, but even if she had, she wondered if police had followed proper protocol. She wanted answers.

When reflecting on the incident, Hillary shared, "After my erroneous arrest, I felt violated, cheated, wronged, and afraid."

The weekend after the incident, Hillary ran into her friend Jovita Moore, a prominent Atlanta TV news anchor. She told her the story and asked if she could help. Jovita wasn't sure it would get aired because a similar story had been done recently, but she gave it a try anyway. The story ended up appearing on the news at 5 p.m., 6 p.m., 11 p.m., and over the weekend. Her receipts from paying her tickets and Moore's investigation proved that Hillary did not have a suspended license, nor did she even have an outstanding ticket. Jovita called the police station and asked what they do when someone has a suspended license. They said they give a verbal warning, a written warning, and the last resort is to arrest the driver.

I met Hillary a few years after this happened, and she told me this story when I told her I was writing *The Joy of Thriving While Black*. I was in shock.

Though the news story made her feel vindicated, Hillary received neither apology nor redress. She just hoped the story could play a small role in giving the police pause before they did this to anyone else.

Sometimes activism can be a simple as that—just telling your story.

WE WILL BE HEARD

I met Millicent Johnnie around 2008–2009 in Atlanta. She and I were both dancers, and we met through mutual friends. Before I knew anything else about her, I knew that she could dance her ass off. I am generally terrible at remembering years and dates, but I know that Millie, which is what family and close friends call her, was in Atlanta in 2009 because my mother passed away that year. She gave me a gift bag of candles and books that helped her make it through her own mother's passing. I will never forget that kindness. I learned about the events that shaped her personally and professionally when I interviewed her.

Inspired by her mother, Geneva Anne Johnnie, Millicent Johnnie became an agent of change at a young age. It all started when she was working in her mother's gift store, Aunt Jenny's Creole Cottage, in Lafayette, in Southwest Louisiana. Every object in the store was a celebration of Black history and culture from across the entire African Diaspora. It was a visual representation of the pride her mother felt in her culture, and she passed that down to Millie.

Her mother had opened the shop after retiring from teaching. She owned one of only two Black businesses on Main Street. Millie explained, "The shop's location was significant because it was on the parade route. Historically, Black people weren't allowed to have a parade route, go to the parades downtown, let alone own a business there." Millie's mother fought hard to secure that business; this act of courage created a role model for those looking up to her, including Millie.

Millie was a gifted salesperson, though she didn't think of herself as that at all. She saw herself as a storyteller who loved bringing the objects in the store to life. According to Millie, "I had this habit. It didn't matter what you picked up in the store; I would tell you the backstory. I would tell you where it came from, why it was important, and why you needed it." She loved history, especially the Creole history behind many of the items in the store.

One day, a woman who, unbeknownst to Millie, was a television producer, came into the store and took an interest in a gold-plated cup from Kenya. That woman, Marie Washum, was so impressed with Millie that she invited her to host the pilot of a local social justice television show, *Those Tender Years*. The show was on the Acadiana Open Channel. She and her coproducer, John Bess, liked the pilot so much that Millie became a permanent host and continued to host it throughout high school. During her tenure in the role, Millie covered many important issues and events, including the Million Man March, interviewing one of the organizers, Bishop Stallings. The network's programming was progressive and forward-thinking and laid the foundation for her later work as an artist and organizer.

Every Sunday, she recorded the show live, and at the end, people had the opportunity to call in. By the second year, the series was steadily gaining traction and popularity. Members of the Ku Klux Klan got wind of it and began prank calling the show. When Millie was undeterred, they started hanging out in the lobby of the studio or in the front of the building. She had to walk past them to get to her car.

As terrifying as this may seem, Millie wasn't afraid. Her mother was a prominent member of the community—an organizer, historian, and storyteller with a strong crew of friends. Millicent always felt protected. Looking back on it, Millie recounted, "I wasn't raised to be afraid of white people. I was raised to be cautious and careful. I was raised to pose questions and keep my head on a swivel, but never to feel subordinate or inferior."

When reflecting on this experience, Millicent shared, "I trace my professional determination and commitment to social issues in Black culture to this early opposition." This experience emboldened her and sealed her commitment to social justice and telling Black stories through mediums ranging from dance to film.

In 2020, Millie earned her MFA in film with a focus on producing. Film school wasn't easy. The Hollywood "formula," as Millie described it, attempts to dictate how you write. The goal is to create a hit whether or not the project fulfills the writer and director's vision. Millie quickly concluded, "I was going to be pushing a ball up a hill in almost any space that I didn't create myself." That is why she became a producer. Her view is that "when storytelling is centered and rooted in whiteness, we disappear." After a twenty-year career as an artist, she wanted to be in the most powerful position possible to control the narrative.

Millie's work is in the spirit of feminist writer and activist Audre Lorde, who stated, "I have come to believe over and over again that what is most important to me must be spoken, made verbal and shared, even at the risk of having it bruised or misunderstood."[25]

Millie continues to create powerful work on the stage and in film, working in front of and behind the camera. She launched Millicent Johnnie Films and moved into an office space in downtown Tallahassee, Florida in February 2021. Her multimedia company creates content that centers artists who identify as Black, Indigenous, and/or People of Color. She has a big vision for her company, including elevating stories from the Gulf South, like in her film *Ma Negresse*.

As a teacher and a culture keeper, Millie has encountered the same problem throughout her life—Black stories and voices being erased. She is an artist and activist on a mission to change that.

BLACK GIRLS MATTER

"We just believe in political action as a tool for the betterment of our community and also this country." That is how Oron-ike Odeleye was raised. When you see something wrong, she

---

25 "Audre Lorde > Quotes > Quotable Quote," Goodreads, accessed January 29, 2021.

explained, you don't point the finger and ask, "Who is going to do something about this?" She just rolls up her sleeves and gets to work.

Thinking back on how I first met Oronike is pretty wild. During the spring of 2007, I was living in Washington, DC and figuring out where I wanted to travel next. I somehow stumbled upon a trip that Oronike was organizing to Panama through the artist residency Taller Portobelo Norte. That trip allowed me to continue my quest to experience carnivals all over the African Diaspora. I hopped on a plane, went to Panama, and met Oronike and the other folks traveling there from all over the country. I moved to Atlanta from DC just a few months after that trip, and Oronike helped welcome me to the city.

Oronike comes from a politically active family. When she was young, her mother worked for the Martin Luther King, Jr. Center in Atlanta. Oronike frequently attended lectures, panels, and movie screenings; she practically lived at the Center. Reflecting on her childhood, Oronike recalls not being allowed to drink Coke products when The Coca-Cola Company still had investments in apartheid South Africa.[26] Her parents had bracelets made and sold them to raise money for anti-apartheid organizations and South African activist Nelson Mandela's release from prison. She recounted that she was constantly "thinking about and hearing about what people were doing to make change wherever they were in the world." Those conversations were a part of the fabric of her life.

That's why, in the summer of 2017, when she heard allegations of singer R. Kelly having a sex cult, she knew she had to

---

26 Bill Sing, "Coca-Cola Acts to Cut All Ties with S. Africa," *Los Angeles Times,* September 18, 1986.

do something. She did her research, and the more she learned, the angrier she became. R. Kelly appeared to be abusing girls right beneath the noses of dozens of bystanders. She simply could not accept that.

It angered and saddened her because, as she expressed it, "Black women and girls do so much for our communities, for our families, for our friends, for our lovers, for political parties, for our churches. We are the worker bees of this country." Kelly's defenders just labeled the girls as "fast," as if their being underage was irrelevant. The message was loud and clear: Those girls' lives didn't matter.

The fact that this was happening in Oronike's hometown of Atlanta made matters even worse. Atlanta is known for having a serious sex trafficking problem. In a 2014 Urban Institute report commissioned by the US Department of Justice, Atlanta ranked number one in the country for sex trafficking.[27] It is speculated that the large international airport and booming convention economy make Atlanta a fruitful market for both pimps and predators. While destroying thousands of lives, the sex trade brought $290 million into Atlanta in 2007. To put that into context, that is more than the revenue from guns and drugs combined.[28]

Oronike did not want to live in a city that was a safe haven for predators like R. Kelly. She wanted to send the message that this was unacceptable: "This is not going to be the norm in our community. Silence makes us all enablers in their abuse." What began as a few calls to DJs requesting that they no longer play R. Kelly's music on the radio turned into a national movement and organization that came to be known

---

27 Deb Belt, "Atlanta Ranked No. 1 for Sex Trafficking; Conventions to Blame?" *Patch*, March 13, 2014.
28 Ibid.

as Mute R. Kelly.[29] Oronike's efforts led to fourteen concerts being canceled, protests in eight cities, and Kelly's music being banned from many radio stations across the nation.[30] In 2019, Oronike received an award from Breakthrough US for her work on the Mute R. Kelly movement. In her acceptance speech, she shared, "This work has shown me that all of us have to be activists everywhere we are, all the time, every day if we want to create the kind of world where our children are safe. I believe that, together, we can build this world."[31] Oronike is modest about her role in cofounding the Mute R. Kelly movement; to her, she was just doing her part, doing what needed to be done.

My admiration of Oronike's power, commitment, and leadership has only grown since we met in 2007. I am grateful for her reminder that we all "have to be activists everywhere we are, all the time."

It is impossible to talk about thriving while Black without considering the simple but powerful statement by civil rights giant Fannie Lou Hamer, "Nobody's free until everybody's free."[32] America was not created for Black folks to thrive; it was built on our unpaid labor and subjugation. That was the hand we were dealt, but with thoughtful, deliberate action, it can change. Doing nothing engenders feelings of hopelessness. Taking action can lead to change and make us feel more powerful. These stories invite us to consider how we can all be activists so we can thrive together.

---

29 "The #MuteRKelly Team," #MuteRKelly, accessed January 29, 2021.
30 Ibid.
31 Oronike Odeleye, "Oronike Odeleye Acceptance Speech — Inspiration Awards 2019," Breakthrough US, April 30, 2019, YouTube video, 1:41.
32 Jon Greig, "'Nobody's Free until Everybody's Free': Fannie Lou Hamer's Legacy Is More Important Now Than Ever," Blavity, October 07, 2019.

QUESTIONS FOR REFLECTION

1. What kind of world do you want to live in? What small action can you take to move toward that world?
2. What can you no longer accept that you would like to change?
3. Who do you look up to for the positive change they have made in the world?
4. How can you stand up for yourself more?
5. Who believes what you believe and can be your ally?

CHAPTER 3

PRIDE

---

*"I find, in being black, a thing of beauty: a
joy; a strength; a secret cup of gladness."*

—OSSIE DAVIS

Black folks who thrive embrace and celebrate their Blackness and African ancestry. However, that is not always easy when starting at a young age, children are bombarded with messages that to be Black is to be inferior. In 1940, two Black social scientists helped uncover the impact this has on Black children.

Dr. Mamie Phipps Clark and Dr. Kenneth Clark, born in 1917 and 1914, respectively, earned their bachelor's and master's degrees from Howard University. Together, they became the first African Americans to earn doctorate degrees in psychology from Columbia University. Mamie worked with children in an all-Black nursery school, which inspired her master's thesis, "The Development of Consciousness of Self in Negro Pre-School Children." Her husband, Kenneth, joined her in exploring this theme, and their work led them to develop the seminal "doll" experiment in 1940.[33]

If you're not familiar with the experiment, let me paint a picture. The Clarks placed two identical dolls, except for skin color, in front of a Black child. They then asked a series of questions and told the child to point to the doll that represented their response. The questions began with which doll was white and which was Black. Easy enough. Then the questions progressed to which doll was pretty, nice, and clean. You guessed it; the children all pointed to the white doll. For which doll is ugly, bad, and dirty, they pointed to the Black doll. When children grow up with these ideas, they pass them on to their children. Colorism and self-hatred are perpetuated generation after generation.

If that isn't tragic enough, since 1940, the study has been continuously repeated with children from diverse backgrounds all over the world. The results are always the same.

Fortunately, powerful forces are working to change that narrative to one of Black pride and self-love. I am so grateful for all the people, especially artists, who reflect the beauty of Blackness in their work. One of those artists is Dr. Fahamu Pecou.

AFRO-OPULENT

Dr. Fahamu Pecou's work is literally everywhere—in museums from Seattle to Paris, on college and university campuses, and hanging on walls in films and television shows, including HBO's *Between the World and Me*, *Black-ish*, and *The Chi*.[34] In his visually stunning multidisciplinary work,

---

33   "Mamie Phipps Clark, PhD, and Kenneth Clark, PhD," American Psychological Association, accessed March 4, 2021.

34   "The Official Website of Visual / Performing Artist & Scholar," Fahamu Pecou Art, accessed March 4, 2021.

Fahamu is as adept at sampling and remixing as the most skilled hip-hop DJ. His work moves freely between responding to and critiquing popular culture while also making connections to ancient ideas. Everything about Fahamu's work reflects pride in his race, culture, and ancestry. His work is vibrant, bold, contemplative, and decidedly Black.

I originally met Fahamu through Oronike Odeleye when I moved to Atlanta in 2007. I naturally fell into the ecosystem they already inhabited, which consisted of art openings, dancing to house music, going to live concerts, and voraciously consuming all that is Black and beautiful.

For Fahamu, "thriving" is about "fully expressing, fully articulating, fully performing who you are, without reservation." That is a mouthful, but as an artist, PhD, and scholar, he has a lot to say through his words and his work. One example is his project TRAPADEMIA III: 7 African Powers. In this series of paintings, he continues to explore Blackness by drawing "parallels to African spiritual and ancestral presence."[35] In his work, he directs the viewer away from "viewing Black people solely as victims of trauma and suffering by revealing the deeper legacy of Black identity…transforming these often misinterpreted bodies into expressions of beauty, pride, and majesty."[36] One painting in the series, *Ade All Day*, depicts Fahamu in a white T-shirt emblazoned with the word "KING" on the front in colorful, graphically patterned lettering. Around his head is a crown of woven cotton plants, which evokes Black people's history as enslaved people.

The largest exhibit of his work I have seen in person was at the High Museum of Art in Atlanta in 2015. All the work was

---

35 "Trapademia III: 7 African Powers," Fahamu Pecou Art, accessed March 3, 2021.

36 Ibid.

stunning, but I was most intrigued by Sound Station, 2015.[37] At this literal station in the middle of one of the galleries, you could put on headphones and press the buttons to create mixes of Aimé Césaire's poetry with hip hop lyrics, beats, and other sound effects. By then, I had seen many of Fahamu's paintings and heard him rap and do performance art pieces. I remember thinking, *Is there anything this guy can't do*? There is only one way to describe how I felt coming to face to face with his paintings that were over four times my size. I felt proud.

In 2016, I went to Fahamu's opening celebration for his mural at the Martin Luther King, Jr. MARTA station in Atlanta.[38] The mural, emblazoned with the words "Rise Above," depicts a Black man jumping, taking flight, face gazing toward the sky, heart lifted as his arms and legs float behind him. Multicolored birds appear to fly from his feet in the opposite direction from the way the man is moving. Fahamu and I chatted for a moment at the opening, and he told me he wanted to talk later about a project he was working on. I was intrigued.

We spoke on the phone a few days later, and he shared his vision for his short film, *Emmett Still. Emmett Still* is about "a day in the precarious life of a young Black man. This is a world where a random encounter with police can quickly turn into a life-or-death situation. Ultimately, he discovers strength and assurance in the power and beauty of his ancestors."[39] Fahamu wanted me to draw from my experience with Afro-Cuban Orisha dance to do some choreography for the

37 "Imagining New Worlds: Wifredo Lam, José Parlá, Fahamu Pecou High Museum of Art," High Museum of Art, accessed March 4, 2021.

38 Kimber Williams, "Art for All: Fahamu Pecou Takes His Painting to the People," *Emory News Center*, June 30, 2016.

39 Fahamu Pecou, "Emmett Still: A Short Film by Fahamu Pecou," YouTube video, 15:13.

film. I was immediately excited and honored. When I asked him when the filming would take place, he said, "Friday." That was in two days! He cast the entire film organically and intuitively with family and people he already knew. It was one of the most fun, creative, and generative collaborations I have ever been a part of as a performer.

Emmett Still was one of the pieces that Fahamu created for his dissertation project, "Do or Die: Affect, Ritual, Resistance." The name is a play on the name of Emmett Till, the fourteen-year-old boy lynched in Mississippi in 1955 for allegedly whistling at a white woman.[40] The film is complex, as is all of Pecou's work. One of the most striking things about the piece is the masquerade Fahamu cocreated with Atlanta artist Grace Kisa. Generally, masquerades represent ancestral spirits that are to be respected and venerated. In *Emmett Still*, the strips of fabric hanging from the cowrie shell mask and hood bear the names of slain Black people, including Amadou Diallo, Philando Castille, Sandra Bland, Eric Garner, Freddie Gray, and Tamir Rice. This masquerade both honors them and metaphorically invites them back to commune with us.

Though *Emmett Still* is set in the context of police brutality, it has a decidedly hopeful and transcendent tone. Fahamu explained:

"Within this country you will always find examples of us thriving, despite what was going on around us. And I think that this is one of the more magical and beautiful and transformative realizations about Blackness. Blackness is not the struggle; it is the fact that we can exist and express and be dynamic in spite of that."

---

40 "The Murder of Emmett Till," PBS, accessed March 4, 2021.

In doing my research on Fahamu, I came across his review of *Black Is King*, Beyoncé's 2020 Disney film. Disney describes the film as being "a tale about a young king's transcendent journey through betrayal, love, and self-identity. *Black Is King* is an affirmation of a grand purpose, with lush visuals that celebrate Black resilience and culture. The film highlights the beauty of tradition and Black excellence."[41] I had not seen the film yet, but we chatted about it for a bit. Beyoncé has sold millions of albums and has 165 million Instagram followers, so she has a lot of eyes on her. In her work, she is elevating ancient and modern African culture, iconography, and contemporary African artists themselves. Millions of Black people, including children, saw the film and will connect the dots: Black and African are beautiful and something to be proud of because Beyoncé says so. Representation by one of the most influential people on the planet matters.

Black Is King is on the Disney Channel, which makes it that much more spectacular and subversive. Think about it: One of Disney's most successful films that references a South African fable, stars animals, not people. So, as Fahamu stated so eloquently, Beyoncé "appropriated Disney's appropriation and gave it back to us Black as fuck." As he declared on his blog, *Black Is King* is "an epically gorgeous, beautifully articulated, masterfully produced portrait of Afro-opulence!"[42] I feel the same way about Fahamu's work.

Another artist who uses her work to preserve and celebrate Black stories and ancestry is Charmaine Minniefield.

---

41 "A Film by Beyoncé Black Is King," Disney, accessed March 4, 2021.
42 Fahamu Pecou, "Regal Is as Regal Does…," *Art. Rap. Scholarshit*, August 04, 2020.

REMEMBRANCE

On March 16, 2020, Charmaine missed boarding her flight by fifteen minutes. That day, she and her family were supposed to return to the United States from The Gambia, West Africa. Due to all the new travel restrictions resulting from the coronavirus pandemic, she needed to get to the airport hours earlier than was customary. She was placed on a flight a few days later, but it was canceled. She was forced to reckon with the fact that she could not return to the US for the foreseeable future.

Charmaine, a multimedia artist, had originally gone to Senegal to build a second residence where she could create an artist exchange program. She took a weekend trip to The Gambia, a skinny country surrounded by Senegal. "We love The Gambia. It's like Jamaica in many ways. It's tropical, English speaking, and they really identify with reggae music, so reggae is everywhere." The Gambia is a stunning country and a popular vacation destination for West Africans. Upon arriving, Charmaine could see why. She never ended up returning to Senegal and remained in quarantine in The Gambia with her daughter for eight months.

The beginning of the pandemic changed everything for Charmaine. As she described it, "All of my work in Atlanta shifted. Everything was canceled. I lost murals. I was supposed to be awarded something in Denver that was postponed. I have tenants in my home, so I thought, *What am I rushing back for*?"

Everywhere she looked, Charmaine saw women who looked just like her draped in the blue indigo dyed fabric popular in the country. Once she adjusted to the idea that she couldn't return home for a while, she created her own artist residency in The Gambia to search for her ancestors. This required her to reimagine her artistic practice because there was limited access to art supplies in The Gambia, like canvas and fine papers. She turned to indigenous practices and customs familiar to her from her upbringing. She explained:

"This process of discovery was guidance from my ancestors to come back home to Africa and my family."

One of the major works put on hold was her installation to honor eight hundred recently discovered unmarked graves in Oakland Cemetery's African American burial grounds in Atlanta. Her work, *Remembrance as Resistance*, celebrates the Ring Shout, a traditional African American worship practice. According to the project website, "From its roots in West Africa, the Ring Shout was reborn during enslavement in the West in resistance to laws which prohibited those enslaved from gathering, except for worship, and forbid any form of cultural expression not in service to the enslavers, including drumming."[43]

During a Ring Shout, congregants would gather in a circle in Praise Houses to stomp and shout, performing full-body rhythmic movement. The stomping on the wooden floors and clapping recreated the sound of drumming. These secret gatherings worked to preserve rituals, prayers, and traditions. These small clandestine worship spaces were the first Black churches in the Western world.

Remembrance as *Resistance* was originally scheduled to open on June 19, 2020, so it had to be postponed to 2021. Charmaine's work is all about reclaiming stories of her

---

43 "Remembrance as Resistance: Preserving Black Narratives," Flux Projects, accessed March 4, 2021.

ancestors to counter the historic erasure of Black people from the history of the Americas. Nothing says "erasure" like being buried without a trace. That reminds me of actress Viola Davis' response to a common question:

"People ask me all the time, What kind of stories do you want to tell, Viola? And I say, Exhume those bodies, exhume those stories—the stories of the people who dreamed big and never saw those dreams come to fruition."[44]

For Charmaine, remembrance is not only an act of resistance but an act of pride.

Charmaine is a culture keeper, a griot, if you will. She serves as the eyes and ears of the community and is an artist and teacher. Artists and culture keepers remind us of all we have to be proud of. During a recent visit to her Facebook page, I felt like I should have been taking notes. During a brief scroll, I saw a post about the HBO documentary *Black Art: In the Absence of Light*, an article about the aesthetics of Blackness, and a piece about why lawyer and activist Bryan Stevenson believes art can help us confront the challenges of racism. Even 4,500 miles away, she was still teaching me by proudly showing beautiful representations of Blackness.

SAY IT LOUD!

When my mother was growing up in the fifties, Black people were rarely on television. When it happened, it was a big deal. People would pick up the phone and call their friends saying, "Black people on TV! Black people on TV!" Sixty-plus years

---

44 Angelique Jackson and Jazz Tangcay, "Viola Davis and Stacey Abrams on Oscar Season, Politics and Wielding Their Power as Black Women," *Variety*, February 17, 2021.

later, we are still struggling for representation that makes us proud, reflects our beauty, and affirms our joy.

When Chadwick Boseman, star of *Black Panther*, gave his 2019 acceptance speech at the Screen Actors Guild Awards, he said:

"We know what it's like to be told there's not a screen for you to be featured on or a stage for you to be featured on. We know what it's like to be the tail and not the head."[45]

When Chadwick Boseman passed away, I started learning more about his life and legacy. He refused to play any character he wasn't proud to portray. Over his short career, he was in many films, playing giants like James Brown, Jackie Robinson, and Thurgood Marshall. He knew that "representation matters."

I am so proud to be Black. I love the way we walk and dance. I love the way we clap and stomp when we laugh. I love our music, our art, our musicians, and our artists. I love our language and the way we can communicate so much with one word. *Bruh. Lissen. Chiiiile!* I love our hair and our style. I love the way we make something out of nothing. Cuisine out of scraps. Quilts out of hand-me-downs and throwaways.

I long for the day that every Black child grows up feeling Black and proud, and the doll experiment becomes a strange relic of the past.

---

45   Chadwick Boseman, "Black Panther: Award Acceptance Speech 25th Annual SAG Awards," TNT, YouTube video, 5:27.

QUESTIONS FOR REFLECTION

1. When did you first learn what it meant to be "Black"? How did you feel?
2. How do you define your Blackness?
3. What about "Blackness" are you proud of?
4. Who do you look up to for how they portray Black people in media or the arts?
5. What do you want to teach the Black children in your life about their racial, cultural, and political identity?

PART II

"If you want to go fast, go alone; if you want to go far, go together."

—AFRICAN PROVERB

CHAPTER 4

COMMUNITY

———

"Ubuntu is very difficult to render into a Western language. It speaks of the very essence of being human. It is to say, 'My humanity is inextricably bound up in yours.'"

—DESMOND TUTU

I learned from experience, my clients, and my research that the happiest people in the world, those who are thriving, are a part of close-knit communities. Running for eighty years, the Harvard Study of Adult Development is one of the world's longest studies of adult life. According to an article in *The Harvard Gazette* covering the study, "Close relationships, more than money or fame, are what keep people happy throughout their lives. Those ties protect people from life's discontents, help to delay mental and physical decline, and are better predictors of long and happy lives than social class, IQ, or even genes."[46] That's not surprising. The sense of belonging is a fundamental need that not only makes us feel good emotionally but also keeps us safe, literally.

A community is made up of people who have common values, attitudes, and goals and agree to support one another. It can include family members, friends, and people with whom we work and volunteer. We can also build community through school, sports, or faith communities. There are endless places we can build community with like-minded people and advance our goals. It used to be that community members lived in close physical proximity to one another, but technologies like cell phones, social media, and video conferencing have changed that.

The jobs I have had over the years provided a strong sense of community. I've loved every single one and made friends with great colleagues along the way. Because I really believed in the missions, I was always fully invested, leading panels, mentoring younger staff, and joining affinity groups. It was in my best interest to do all that I could to make the places I worked as good as they could be.

For most of my career, I went to a physical location to work with people who had similar values and a shared mission. That all changed in 2015 when I launched my first business, a nonprofit consulting practice. I had to wake up every day, motivate myself to work, write proposals, and devise client solutions with no one to bounce ideas off of besides my clients. It was hard and lonely. I only lasted for a year because I yearned for the community provided by a full-time job.

46 Liz Mineo, "Good Genes Are Nice, but Joy Is Better," *The Harvard Gazette*, April 11, 2017.

My next role was at iMentor, but our office was based in New York and I worked remotely from Atlanta. I am extremely extroverted and was desperate for some place to go, connect with new people, and exchange ideas organically. I also wanted to expand my networks beyond the nonprofit community I had been immersed in for twenty-five years. I needed a new professional community, which inspired me to join The Gathering Spot (TGS).

WHY WE GATHER

Joining TGS in 2017 was a game changer for me personally and professionally. When I first joined, I was still working at iMentor. It gave me a place to go when I wasn't traveling to connect with people locally. The physical space is beautifully designed, open, and bathed in natural light. Just being there brings me joy.

From the moment I walk in the door, I get a boost of energy. I am always greeted by name with a smile and can count on receiving at least one hug. Just walking from the door to wherever I might decide to work for the day, I have several conversations that remind me of my purpose and fuel my work for the day. I love the expression, "If you can't see it, you can't be it." Being at TGS surrounded by bright, ambitious entrepreneurs at various stages of their journey reminds me that I can thrive as an entrepreneur too.

So many avenues have opened up for me professionally because of my membership at TGS. That is where I met Morgan Wider, author of *The Worthy Wardrobe*. She told me about the Creator Institute, which supported her in writing her book. I followed her journey to becoming an author, which made me feel like I could do it too. I also filmed my book trailer at TGS in October 2020, and that very same day,

I met Lee Ashby Watts, a marketing consultant who helped me refine my brand identity.

Over the years, I have enjoyed the structured programming on topics ranging from tax tips for entrepreneurs, understanding public relations, creating strong LinkedIn profiles, and how to maintain mental health during the coronavirus pandemic. It has become a one-stop shop for almost anything I need as an entrepreneur, with an emphasis on the information and opportunities especially relevant to Black folks.

For every event focused on business, there is also something fun and entertaining, from spades nights to film screenings and chess lessons. One of my favorite events was a group outing to see Alvin Ailey preceded by a pre-show dinner at TGS.

On February 26, 2020, NBC Nightly News did a piece on TGS while I was there in the restaurant. A reporter asked what TGS meant to me and thrust a microphone toward me. My off-the-cuff reply was simple and honest: "I want to be a part of the movement that says, 'This is the place for Black entrepreneurs to be, thrive, and support each other."[47]

My last day going to TGS before the pandemic was Friday, March 13, 2020. I am not superstitious, but I knew I would always remember that date. It was the last time I would be with a group of like-minded people in person for a long time.

THRIVING THROUGH DISTANCE

The coronavirus pandemic created a major barrier to building and maintaining community. It's funny to recall that

---

47   "Tech Industry Fuels Reverse Migration for Black Americans (Part 2)," NBC Universal, February 26, 2020, 1:28.

we thought it would only last a couple of weeks. In his book, *Together: The Healing Power of Human Connection in a Sometimes Lonely World,* Dr. Vivek H. Murthy described our predicament so well: "In the first weeks of 2020, the COVID-19 pandemic turned physical human contact into a potentially mortal threat. The public health imperative was clear: To save lives, we'd need to radically increase the space between us."[48] For an extrovert like me, that was a tough pill to swallow.

Murthy served as the nineteenth Surgeon General of the United States of America. As Surgeon General, he had to devise strategies to address many public health crises, including the rise in opioid abuse. Over the course of his career, he learned there was something deeper, more insidious underlying these conditions. He explained:

"Loneliness ran like a dark thread through many of the more obvious issues that people brought to my attention, like addiction, violence, anxiety, and depression."[49]

The antidote to loneliness is, of course, authentic relationships and community.

The first few weeks of the pandemic are a bit of a blur. A month after we began sheltering in place, the fear of isolation began setting in. I knew that other people were feeling the same way and looking for comfort and community. I started thinking about how I could be of service from the safety of my home. I decided to offer free live, guided meditations over Zoom. People turned out in droves.

---

48   Vivek Murthy, *Together: The Healing Power of Human Connection in a Sometimes Lonely World* (New York: HarperCollins Publishers, 2020), xiii.

49   Ibid, xix.

Much to my surprise, several of the attendees later hired me to lead guided meditations and well-being check-ins for organizations as diverse as a law firm, a real estate investment company, a "mommy and me" group, and nonprofits around the country. I led a dozen of these engagements throughout 2020. Well-being check-ins, including gentle yoga and meditation, eventually became a core offering of my coaching practice.

The well-being check-ins were as good for me as they were for my participants. They helped me feel connected, purposeful, and of service during a really challenging time. I knew that in order to survive the pandemic and the necessary sheltering in place, I would need to create an additional means of connecting with my community virtually.

I was fortunate to have friends like Blythe Keeler Robinson, who became a key member of my virtual Corona Survival Crew.

MY SISTER'S KEEPER

When Blythe thinks of "thriving," she thinks about "well-being and connectedness." She defines "well-being" broadly: "I mean mental, physical…what are my relationships like? I'm intentionally seeking positivity in my life."

Blythe Keeler Robinson moved to Atlanta from Miami in 2013 to become CEO of Sheltering Arms Early Education & Family Centers, one of Atlanta's largest and most respected nonprofits. I met her in 2013 at an event organized by the executive search firm that had recruited her for the role. Twenty people whom the firm had previously recruited, including me, were invited to lunch to introduce her to other leaders in Atlanta's nonprofit community. I remember how excited I was to meet her and see another Black woman in such a prominent leadership role. Blythe was poised, elegant, and radiated confidence. She was impeccably dressed, with graceful mannerisms and killer dimples. On top of all that, she was warm and friendly.

Atlanta had been a welcoming city to me when I arrived in 2007, and I liked paying it forward whenever I got the opportunity. I had an amazing group of girlfriends in the city whom I thought Blythe would enjoy meeting. Soon after meeting her, my friend Zenith organized a brunch for about a dozen women, and I invited Blythe. That day was the beginning of many new and deepening friendships.

One subset of that friend group was me, Blythe, Zenith, and Qaadirah. We had a lot in common, including the fact that we were all Black, female executive directors/CEOs of children, youth, and education-related nonprofits. We were at the top of our game. Being in the same industry meant that besides our intentional gatherings, our professional worlds collided a lot. We could share what it meant to lead in white spaces and how as Black women, we always had a foot in two worlds—the worlds of our students and the worlds of our board members and donors. We felt the burden and responsibility of operating effectively in both, and it wasn't always easy.

Over the years, we went out for dinners, drinks, brunches, and spa dates. We celebrated key milestones like birthdays and each other's nonprofit fundraisers. Zenith treated us to sumptuous meals in her home, including Thanksgiving dinners. She is such an amazing cook and so good at entertaining. Some of us joked that we felt too intimidated to host after her.

When the four of us met, we were all single and in our thirties, so we compared notes and dating strategies. We shared our frustrations about the dreadful statistics that show that Black professional women are the most likely to remain single. We spent hours discussing, debating, and trying to debunk myths while also finding room for growth. Sometimes we just commiserated. When Qaadirah got engaged, we got together to celebrate and soak in all the sweet details. Blythe, Zenith, and Qaadirah were all at the launch party for my business in January 2020. It felt so good to look out and see them, as they had been a part of my life and leadership journey for about ten years.

Blythe is a connector. She is also that friend who motivates friends to work out and plans workout dates. I will never forget the year that Blythe invited a bunch of girlfriends to join her for a bounce class on her birthday. Imagine twelve forty-plus-year-old women from size four to fourteen doing aerobics in bouncy, springy moon boots. That class nearly gave me a heart attack, but there was Blythe, bouncing away in the front, smiling and full of energy.

When the pandemic hit, Blythe started thinking, "I like alone time, but I recognize when that alone time isn't healthy." Blythe lives by herself, and when she finally wrapped her head around the fact that we would be sheltering in place indefinitely, she thought, "Oh, this is gonna be a problem." As a self-described extroverted introvert, she explained, "I feed off of knowing I have support systems and people I love and care about." So, she set out to create her pandemic support system.

When I received the recurring meeting invite from Blythe for "Tea Time" on March 24, 2020, I was so relieved. Soon after that, she added Thursday morning coffee and Friday happy hours. We even tried singles mixers and formed a movie discussion group. All the members of the groups didn't know each other before quarantine, but our Zoom check-ins bonded us. These connections became central to my own quarantine self-care plan.

We shared so much over the course of a year in quarantine. In many ways, those calls helped us mark the time. When Blythe first scheduled the check-ins, they repeated weekly for a month or so. I remember the panic I felt the Thursday when I didn't see it on my calendar. After setting up new meeting invites repeatedly over the course of the year, she eventually left it open-ended.

A year later, our core Thursday morning crew—me, Blythe, Lisa, Zenith, Che, and Pi—was still going strong. We were each other's anchors as we managed everything the year threw at us. I don't know how I would have survived without them.

THERE IS ALWAYS ROOM FOR ONE MORE BROTHER

It was "just part of the air you breathe." That was how Steven Allwood described the way community was embedded into every aspect of his experience as a Morehouse College student. For him, Morehouse is a part of a long tradition of Black institutions that exist to build the "beloved community" that Dr. Martin Luther King, Jr. popularized.

At Morehouse, Steven had this important ideal drilled into him:

"You may have all these degrees, you may be making money and advancing your career, but if your cousins and them are still struggling, you can't be truly thriving."

Steven attended Morehouse College from 1992 to 1996. The early nineties was an era for a lot of new, rich scholarship that centered on the Black experience. In front of the student union, students broke out into spontaneous debates. Chapel assistants studying to be Christian ministers, members of the National of Islam, and Marxists gathered and discussed voting rights, religion, or whatever was the subject of the day. During the debates, the students would start pulling books out of their backpacks to back up their arguments. They were passionate about their beliefs, and their opinions reflected the diversity of the student body. Steven was so captivated by these exchanges that he was sometimes late to class.

One of the formal centers of Morehouse life was the King Chapel, a dignified place full of grandeur, pomp, and circumstance. The room is draped in maroon and white, the college's colors, and flags that represent all the countries that Morehouse students hail from. The chapel is home to a pipe organ that boasts an impressive 5,209 pipes.[50] Every Thursday at 11 a.m., the students and faculty gathered in the King Chapel for the Crown Forum to hear various speakers and presenters who came from all over the world to address the Morehouse community.

When it got close to graduation, Steven distinctly remembers looking around the chapel, trying to cement the memory of the experience into his brain. Once, he was seated in the balcony, probably not paying much attention to what was happening during the Crown Forum because he was so deep in thought about his college career. There are 2,501 seats in the chapel. The "extra" seat represents the idea that "there is always room for one more brother." As Steven looked around, he realized that might be the last time he sat in a room of that many Black men. However, he was comforted by the likelihood that most of their lives would turn out well. They had received a quality education and spent four years at a college that affirmed them and valued their lives as Black men.

---

50 "Wicks Organ Co. (Opus 5874, 1982)," Organ Historical Society, accessed January 29, 2021.

Steven had no idea at the time that he would end up back at Morehouse in 2017 working in the counseling center, eventually becoming its director.

As a clinical psychologist, one of the issues Steven supports students with is grief. The first thing he was trained to do when a student loses a loved one is to help them activate their support network. In the best circumstances, Steven worked with students who had developed strong friendship networks. When they were grieving, they could activate their network, share their troubles, and receive encouragement and support. However, he was shocked whenever students went into the office following a tragedy, not having told anyone. They, too, had friends but had learned that a "strong man" does not share emotional vulnerability. They were embarrassed to admit to their friends that they were grieving. A smaller number of students that Steven worked with could only identify a girlfriend as someone they could turn to for support. For Steven, this was cause for concern because, he thought, "if that relationship ends, you're screwed."

Being a psychologist who was also raised by a therapist, Steven grew up understanding the importance of cultivating authentic male friendships. He knew that friendship was key to thriving. But when his wife asked for a divorce in 2017 after sixteen years of marriage, his ability to build strong, supportive friendships was put to the test.

Steven had become a soccer fan around 2010 when the World Cup was in South Africa. He got more and more into soccer over the years. When it was announced that Atlanta was getting a team, he was thrilled to have a hometown team to root for. Not being a huge "sports guy," he assumed he would go to a few games a year—until he found out there were official supporter groups. He thought that by joining, he could meet some new people, which would give him a new social outlet.

The group that immediately captured his imagination was called Footie Mob, inspired by the Atlanta-based hip-hop group Goodie Mob. According to their mission statement: "Footie Mob's first goal is to grow and diversify the soccer fan base in Atlanta. Our second goal is to bring Atlanta culture to MLS. Atlanta has long been a home to the arts: whether it's Margaret Mitchell, Alice Walker, George Pemberton, Outkast or Martin Luther King."[51]

As he got to know the members of the club, he fell in love with the entire game-day experience. Because the Footie Mob club was diverse, he got really involved to ensure, he explained, that "it wasn't just cultural appropriation, that we were engaging with the Black community in a meaningful way and increasing the Black membership."

The ending of Steven's marriage changed his relationship to Footie Mob. He expressed, "It became a part of my self-care regimen. It became a way to blow off steam. For four or five hours on a particular Saturday or Sunday, I could be in a space where I could kind of forget about, you know, the shit show in the rest of my life."

One day he was feeling down, but also really grateful for his growing Footie Mob friendships, which was the most diverse friend group he ever had. On a whim, he reached out to its private social media group to share what he was going through and express his gratitude for the group. He said, "Within ten minutes I had, you know, five, six different guys in my inbox just offering support, saying, *I've been through it, It gets better, Do you need a lawyer?, Do you need a shoulder*

---

51   "Mission Statement," Footie Mob, accessed January 29, 2021.

to cry on?" He was completely blown away and humbled by the show of support.

Reflecting on the experience, he told me, "I don't know what I would have done going through a divorce without that. I don't think I would have gone so far as to become suicidal, but I can't even promise that. So, it almost quite literally saved my life."

I could really relate to Steven. My community has held me up during some really difficult times. When my mother passed away in 2009, I was running with Urban Run Club. I remember how good it felt to show up to see my friends every week. It was so grounding at a time when it felt like the ground was shaky beneath my feet. I often ran and cried.

Having my people by my side in the best of times has been equally important. It means everything to know that they are cheering me on. I have experienced that so much over the course of my life, but in 2020, it was critical. I went from launching a business to living in a pandemic and deciding that I should also write *The Joy of Thriving While Black*. I could not have done it without the endless love and support of my community.

QUESTIONS FOR REFLECTION

1. How do you define "community"?
2. Who can you turn to for support any time of day or night?
3. What communities do you belong to, and how do they nurture you?
4. Are there groups that you stay active in purely out of obligation? What would your life look like if you could redirect that time and energy elsewhere?

5. Do you see a need for a type of community that doesn't yet exist? If you feel drawn to create it, who can support you?

CHAPTER 5

SAFE SPACES

---

*"The ache for home lives in all of us. The safe place
where we can go as we are and not be questioned."*

—MAYA ANGELOU

It is not safe to be Black in America.

The killings of Ahmaud Arbery, Breonna Taylor, George
Floyd, and Rayshard Brooks in the spring and summer of
2020 were a painful reminder of that. In June, the country
was on fire. Protests had been going on for weeks straight,
and clashes between police officers and protestors were
increasing. Atlanta was under curfew, and I felt like I was
living in an extremely bad dream.

In fact, two nights in one week, I woke up screaming,
which I didn't remember until my cousin told me the next
morning. I dreamed I had arrived at an airport somewhere
and grabbed a taxi to a hotel. After riding for a while, I sensed
we weren't going in the right direction. I asked my driver
some questions, and he did not respond, which signaled that
something was terribly wrong. I persisted in telling him he

was going the wrong way. When he continued to ignore me, I started yelling for him to stop the car and let me out. I was being kidnapped.

In the next scene, I woke up in the back seat of the taxi to find that the driver had pulled over to take a nap. It would have been the perfect time to escape, except I couldn't move. I started yelling for the police, but then I stopped, thinking, "What if they come and end up shooting me?" I woke up panting in a cold sweat.

By June 2020, the United States had also been under quarantine for three months, so we were living a nightmare within a nightmare. One night, I decided to brave the outdoors for my first socially distanced gathering in my friend Kym's backyard. Because I lived in the suburbs and didn't leave the house much, I wasn't tuned into Atlanta's new curfew hours. I found myself on the highway at 8:56 p.m., still ten minutes away from Kym's house. Next to the highway was a huge billboard lit with red, neon lettering that said, "If you love Atlanta, go home!" This was followed by an announcement that curfew began at 9 p.m. My stomach turned; I had never been more afraid that I would be pulled over in my life.

Looming in my mind was the fact that just two weeks earlier, police officers had forcibly removed two Black Morehouse and Spelman College students from their car and tased and arrested them without explanation.[52] The students were simply stuck in traffic in the middle of the protests downtown. The entire incident was caught on video. One student ended up with a fractured arm and suffered an epileptic seizure.

---

52   Greta Anderson, "Police Fired for Injuring Spelman and Morehouse Students," *Inside Higher Ed*, June 3, 2020.

The fact that I was out on the road in that environment was terrifying. Fortunately, I made it to Kym's house safely.

Later in the month, I decided I was ready to take a little road trip for the sake of my sanity. I booked a stay at The Getaway House outside of Atlanta, which seemed like a safe option. They were operating their tiny house rental business at 50 percent capacity so they could disinfect the houses and create a twenty-four-hour break between guests.

I left home on June 17, 2020 at about 1 p.m for the two-hour drive. My radio was tuned to NPR, as usual. Not long into my ride, a live press conference came on. It was broadcasting the Fulton County district attorney reading the charges against the police officers involved in the killing of Rayshard Brooks. Brooks had been running away from police officers when he was shot in the back.

My first thought was to turn off the radio. I was taking this little trip to clear my mind, so *did I really want to listen to this?* But curiosity combined with the legal geek in me decided to stay tuned in. District Attorney Paul Howard announced eleven charges against former officer Garrett Rolfe, including felony murder and aggravated assault with a deadly weapon. He announced three charges against officer Devin Brosnan, including aggravated assault.[53]

I felt nothing when I heard the charges—not relief, not elation, not happiness. I just felt weary.

But as I continued to drive, I felt lighter and lighter. As the road curved up the North Georgia mountain toward Suches, Georgia, I was forced to slow down, which allowed me to take in the lush scenery. Suches, named after a Cherokee

---

53 Brakkton Booker, "Former Atlanta Police Officer Who Shot Rayshard Brooks Charged with Felony Murder," *NPR*, June 17, 2020.

Chief, is known for its scenic views. With an altitude of three thousand feet, it has clean air and temperatures five to eight degrees cooler than the city. With an average daily temperature of eighty-seven degrees in June in Atlanta, every degree counted.

When I spotted the first sign supporting President Donald Trump's reelection campaign, I was triggered. But the more signs I saw, the less I cared. There is a joke that if you go fifty miles outside of Atlanta in any direction, you go back fifty years in time. No Black person wants to go back fifty years in time, especially in Georgia. But I had consciously chosen this trip eighty miles outside of Atlanta, so I knew what I was in for. Suches is, after all, 97.3 percent white.

The final landmark I hit before turning onto The Getaway House property was a large, dark brown general store and restaurant. Flying in the wind above the establishment was a large American flag and a Trump flag. Let me repeat that, *a Trump flag.* I exhaled deeply as I continued my drive onto the property, praying that my lodging was not in view of that place.

As I began to wind my way through the property, I felt relieved. Something about a tiny house brings me joy, but an entire community of them? Now that's just heaven. Heading up there, though, I was worried that the houses would be far apart, I might feel too isolated and hence, unsafe. However, I saw they were just far apart enough to give you privacy but close enough to create a sense of community among guests. I continued to drive among the dozens of houses looking for mine. I turned the last corner and spotted my cabin. Right across the road, I saw one of the best things I could see deep into Trump country—Black people!

I pulled up, got out of my car, and waved to them exuberantly like I was greeting old friends. "Boy, am I happy to see you!" I said.

"Me too!" they yelled back.

Those were the first words spoken between three Black people meeting for the very first time, and they held so much meaning. Seeing each other made us feel safe. We chatted for a bit, and I learned that the couple was visiting for the weekend from Charlotte. When the wife saw my yoga mat, she mentioned she loved yoga. So, before entering my cabin, I invited them to practice yoga with me outside the next morning.

I walked into my tiny house, put my stuff down, and exhaled. I had successfully driven while Black through north Georgia. I had arrived safely and met some friendly Black people. I knew my time there would be lovely.

The threat to Black safety is not only physical but also psychological. Being Black in majority-white spaces can subject you to intense scrutiny, microaggressions, and questions about whether you belong or have a right to be there. I have benefitted from many organizations and programs created to mitigate those threats.

FIVE PERCENT BLACK

In 1988, the summer after my junior year in high school, I left my home on the South Side of Chicago to attend a program called "Summer College" at Cornell University. It was an opportunity to experience the campus, take classes, and earn college credit—basically a chance to "try before you buy" the full Cornell undergraduate experience.

While I was at Summer College, I encountered some rising Cornell freshmen who were in a program called "COSEP."

In 1963, Cornell President James Perkins had launched the Committee on Special Educational Projects (COSEP) to increase African American student enrollment and provide them with support services. It was the first program of its kind at a major American university.[54] I didn't know much about COSEP; all I knew was the cool kids were in the program and I wanted in. Because the students I met in COSEP were Black and Brown, I just assumed that if I was admitted to Cornell, I would get an invitation.

When I returned home at the end of Summer College, I applied to Cornell early decision, got accepted, and waited and waited for my COSEP invitation. When it never arrived, I called the Minority Affairs office to inquire about what I assumed was my misplaced invitation. Thinking back on it, I must have sounded extremely entitled.

The first question the person on the other end of the line asked was, "How do you even know about that program?" I explained and was then told the number of slots was limited and I had not been invited. I just could not wrap my head around that. To me, attending Cornell in the fall went hand in hand with participating in COSEP over the summer. I just had to get in! As fate would have it, a couple of slots opened up from students who had planned to go but backed out at the last minute.

During my pre-freshman COSEP summer, I made great friends who would remain friends throughout my undergraduate career. I took classes and learned things like time management and built relationships with the staff of the COSEP office. I was especially fond of Elisa Johnson, the Office Assistant of Minority Education Affairs. She took her

---

54   George Lowery, "A Campus Takeover That Symbolized an Era of Change," *Cornell Chronicle*, April 16, 2009.

job seriously and really cared about us. The entire experience made the transition to my freshman year that much easier. When I stepped on campus in the fall of 1989, I felt like I belonged. The summer after my freshman year, I remained on campus as a peer counselor for the incoming COSEP students, which was an honor and a good gig.

One of the COSEP funding innovations was to pay students who led campus organizations through work-study, recognizing that a disproportionate number of students of color had to work in college. If they could do things they loved that benefitted the entire campus community, it was a win-win. Working would deepen ties with the university and increase retention and graduation rates. This meant that for two years, I got paid to be codirector of Uhuru Kuumba Dance Ensemble. In addition to dancing and doing choreography, my codirector and I also oversaw the audition process, managed the budget, helped plan the annual concerts, created flyers, sold tickets, managed the venue, and made our own costumes. It was a robust position for which I was thrilled to get paid. The experience also helped cement my role and identity as a campus leader.

Another institution that meant a lot to me was my dorm, Ujamaa. Student of color-led organizations met, had important conversations about campus life, and planned protests there. Hundreds of us also gathered weekly in front of one small television to watch *The Cosby Show* and *A Different World*. None of these spaces excluded white people. They just focused on the experiences of people of color.

Some white students questioned the legitimacy of programs like Ujamaa. The idea of Black and Brown students gathering was threatening. We were labeled as separatists, but we knew better. Implicit in their critique was questions like: Why do they deserve all this special treatment? Isn't it enough that they got admitted due to affirmative action, taking the spot of some more deserving white person? Why even attend Cornell if all they want to do is segregate themselves?

My reaction ranged from wanting to fight to a simple eye roll. Black students were about five percent of the Cornell student body, and the college was founded when our ancestors were still enslaved. Yeah, that reeks of privilege.

Scholar Marcia Chatelain addresses this reaction pointedly when she says:

"When critics mock students for wanting safe spaces, they often argue that political correctness is undermining education and that students today are 'too sensitive.' Rarely do I ever hear any curiosity about what students are seeking shelter from."[55]

Being together fortified us to face the extra burdens placed on us in the broader campus community.

COSEP and Ujamaa were two of many student of color-focused programs I would participate in over the course of my academic career. They were safe spaces dedicated to helping me and my peers thrive, and they meant the world to me.

BETWEEN STARSHINE & CLAY

A poem by Lucille Clifton inspired Octavia Raheem to create Starshine & Clay retreats for women of color to just be, in 2017. The poem asks the reader to celebrate the life that Clifton shaped for herself with no model. Octavia, a yoga

---

55 Marcia Chatelain, "What Mizzou Taught Me," The Chronicle of Higher Education, November 12, 2015.

teacher, author, and educator, first encountered the poem in undergraduate school. By the time she became an Atlanta Public Schools teacher in the late nineties, she had committed it to memory and had it taped to her desk.

In 2016, Octavia opened Sacred Chill West yoga studio on Atlanta's west side. She had been teaching yoga for a long time, but when she opened her yoga studio with her business partner, Black women were coming out in droves. In all her years teaching yoga, she had never taught an overwhelmingly Black class. A woman going to Sacred Chill West was driving all the way from Cumming, Georgia, forty miles away and passing eight yoga studios to get there.

The popular image of someone doing yoga is a thin, white woman twisting her body into the shape of a pretzel. Black women were drawn to Octavia's studio because they could see themselves in her. Many women of color are changing the face and narrative of yoga, but those images have not yet saturated the mainstream. Even though her Black students were in the majority, Octavia noticed that the presence of one or two white women would shift the energy in the room.

One year, Octavia went on a retreat for women of color hosted by one of her mentors, Maya Breuer. It was completely transformative. That was her first time going to a retreat created for Black and Brown women.

Following the experience at that retreat, Octavia set out to create something similar rooted in her experience as a Southern woman. She sought to create a safe space where baggage could be left at the door and women didn't need to perform or do what she described as "some of the things that we normally have to do when we're in survival mode." She envisioned a place where the participants could "exit out of our daily lives to be held and nurtured."

There is a lot of talk and some good work being done to cultivate inclusion in historically white spaces like colleges and universities, corporate C-suites, and boards of directors. But when reflecting on the idea of "inclusion" Octavia pointed out that by definition, "inclusion" means that Black and Brown people are an afterthought. She wanted to create a space where "we were the first thought." Watching her mother and her aunt constantly serving other people, whether it was someone's baby shower or Sunday dinner, also inspired her. She wanted to cultivate the rare space where women like them could be taken care of and put themselves first.

When Octavia talks about Starshine & Clay, you can hear the warmth and love in her voice. She told me that when she's working on Starshine & Clay, it doesn't feel like work, "It feels more like ritual, a deeper sense of service." To create the experiences, she draws from yoga and her experience growing up in church, "You create a sense of fellowship...you welcome the presence of spirit."

Pretty early into the coronavirus pandemic of 2020, Octavia and her business partner decided to shutter the doors of their brick-and-mortar studio. Every time a business that I loved closed, it felt like the aftershock of an earthquake. It was a sad moment for the entire community that would not have this sanctuary to return to when it became safe to gather in person again.

When she announced that she was launching a virtual membership community, my initial response was lukewarm. I had never enjoyed practicing yoga in front of a screen, and given all the time I was already spending on Zoom, I couldn't imagine getting into it. But, in true Octavia fashion, she managed to curate a special, intimate virtual community complete with beautiful digital materials, monthly themes, special guests, weekly streamed classes, and live Zoom retreats that allowed us to connect to one another.

There were some surprising benefits to practicing at home alone. The first was obvious: no one could see me. I could really make my practice 100 percent my own without distracting anyone. One night I was eating some salty caramel ice cream right before class. I know, I know, not the best idea, but it happened. When it was time to practice, I had a little bit left and was about to put it away to finish later. But then I thought, *Hell, I am practicing yoga in front of a screen during a global pandemic, I deserve to finish this ice cream!*

The other thing I enjoyed about practicing alone was setting up my space. When Octavia teaches and leads retreats, she goes all out to make the space beautiful. There are candles, flowers, journals, and pens for everyone, and everyone's mat is laid out neatly with a couple blankets, blocks, and bolsters nearby. I had to try and create this vibe myself before practice. I got started fifteen minutes before class, creating a sacred space for myself. I did it with the care that I would offer if I was preparing the space for someone I loved deeply.

This mirrors Octavia's intention for Starshine & Clay. She describes it as a "soulful practice that honors the simple and profound truth: We are worthy of our own care, love, and devotion." I am so grateful to Octavia for modeling how to create this safe space for myself.

A GATHERING OF POETS

One of the many frustrating things about being Black in majority white spaces, especially educational institutions, is that you're constantly explaining—things that other Black folks would just "get." It's like you're one of the instructors but not getting paid.

That was the experience of poet and educator Derrick Weston Brown when he was earning his master's in fine arts (MFA) in creative writing at American University in Washington, DC. Whenever he shared work in class, his white classmates had so many questions like, "What does that mean?" or "Why is your language so informal?" and then when they "got" it, some assumed that Derrick's views represented all Black people.

Several Black writers and professors took the time to offer Derrick guidance. One was E. Ethelbert Miller, poet, literary activist, Howard University graduate, and DC native. Derrick had the opportunity to interview Miller while working for a newspaper in his hometown of Charlotte, North Carolina. He enjoyed meeting Miller so much that he reached out to him when he was considering graduate school in DC. Miller told Derrick how great it was to be a writer in DC and educated him on all the literary giants who had come through the city.

Professor Keith Leonard, who was in the English department at American University, met with Derrick when he was on sabbatical. They had never met previously, and Leonard took Derrick to lunch, which really blew Derrick's mind. Leonard shared this sage advice: "Find your community in the program, but also find community in the city. As a Black writer, you're going to need that."

For Derrick, thriving while Black means "having a community as a resource that you can help support, and they support you." Nothing nurtured Derrick as a poet like his experience at Cave Canem. He started hearing about this mysterious place for Black poets while he was out and about on the poetry scene in DC. Cave Canem was a poetry workshop that had been around since 1996, and many of the founding members had come from DC. Impressed with his poetry, people started nudging him to apply.

Cave Canem was founded by award-winning poets Toi Derricotte and Cornelius Eady "to remedy the under-representation and isolation of African American poets in the literary landscape…[it] is a home for the many voices of African American poetry and is committed to cultivating the artistic and professional growth of African American poets."[56]

Derrick describes the week-long experience as approximately sixty writers broken into four or five groups. They would work together, taking classes with master poets and just hanging out.

Every retreat began in a welcome circle that included the founders, workshop leaders, staff, and fellows. The attendees were from all walks of life and all over the world. One of the founders, Toi Derricotte, would come out singing and say something like, "Welcome to this space. This is your community. Look around the room. We're all different shades and we're all Black. You're safe here." Every year, those words alone caused some folks to burst into tears. Some people didn't have any support for being a poet from their families or their MFA programs.

While Cave Canem began as a summer retreat for Black poets, it evolved into so much more. Cave Canem alums remain connected and continue to support each other along their journeys as poets. Derrick went three times between 2000 and 2006, and each time, he emerged with more ideas, friends, and books to read. Some people even met their life partners there, later bringing their children to visit.

---

56 "Mission and History," Cave Canem Foundation, accessed January 25, 2021.

When I asked Derrick what it meant to thrive, he explained, "I think imagination is a part of thriving. That means you're looking at all sorts of possibilities." Cave Canem helped fuel Derrick's imagination. It also helped him see the possibility of following in the footsteps of some of his teachers and mentors. The experience allowed him and his peers to unite around being poets and being Black in a place where they could be safe and thrive.

BLACK GIRL MAGIC

I took my first twenty-minute Peloton ride with Alex Toussaint on Saturday, February 29, 2020 at 9:51 a.m. I rode the equivalent of 4.89 miles and burned 152 calories. Nothing was exceptional about that output, but I did it, right in the comfort of my home. There were other metrics I didn't understand, but probably for the first time in my life, I had completed a great cardiovascular workout at home. Little did I know how much I would grow to appreciate this stationary bike in the weeks and months to come.

Soon after I started riding, I discovered a Facebook group called BGM (Black Girl Magic): The Peloton Edition. The group, and even the name, gives me life. Filmmaker Ava Duvernay describes Black Girl Magic as, "a rallying call of recognition. Embedded in the everyday is a magnificence that is so easy to miss because we're so mired in the struggle and what society says we are."[57] There is plenty of "everyday magnificence" in the BGM group, from the encouragement to the tips and the jokes. This powerful support group is led by committed volunteer moderators who engage the group every single day.

---

57   Danielle Young, "6 Ava Duvernay Quotes to Reaffirm Your #Blackgirl-magic," *Essence,* July 2, 2016.

One of them is Michelle Guobadia.

Michelle got her Peloton in June 2018. She loved group fitness, and she didn't know how it would feel working out without other people sweating right beside her. She was taking twenty-eight-dollar fitness classes that she enjoyed, but the classes were almost 100 percent white. She didn't have any terrible experiences, but she just never felt like she belonged. She explained, "I felt like an outsider invading their club…never got the high fives after class and was met with a subtle indifference. Even the instructors were all white, and none of them were shouting out my name in class with encouragement."

When Michelle got her bike, she was going through the breakdown of a relationship that had been unraveling for a while. She immediately got active in the Official Peloton Facebook group and another Black woman sent her a direct message that said, in effect, "We over here," directing Michelle to the BGM: The Peloton Edition group. What made the Black Girl Magic group unique, aside from the demographics, was its intention to be a safe, uplifting space, free from the bullying and trolling that can too often happen online. According to the "About" section of the group, the founders seek to create a "space that is for us, by us, and about us in celebration of our fitness journeys on and off the bike. So, let's share our magic with each other, straighten each other's crowns, and be the iron that sharpens iron on this Peloton journey."[58]

The group's mission is evident day in and day out. The most predominant post is about someone celebrating a

---

58   Black Girl Magic: The Peloton Edition, "About," Facebook, accessed March 15, 2021.

milestone, from reaching one hundred rides, to hitting a new personal record or dropping a few pounds. The response is always thundering virtual applause.

Michelle credits Peloton and BGM with helping her survive the breakup. "I immersed myself into the bike and it was like therapy," she said. She didn't have to get into the details of her situation to fully experience the love and support of the group. It was enough for her to know they were there.

She immediately established herself as a regular, positive contributor to the group. She found so much inspiration and motivation there. One woman who inspired her early on was Sienna, who lives in Brooklyn with her son who has special needs. Sienna worked out and posted regularly. Whenever Michelle saw Sienna's posts, she would think to herself, "She has a special needs kid, she wakes up at the crack of dawn, and she's already got two-and-a-half hours in while I'm still lying in bed. Get up!"

One year after becoming a member of the BGM Facebook group, two of the moderators reached out to Michelle asking if she would become a moderator. At that point, the group had around five thousand members and they needed more help to facilitate and tend to the members' needs. By January 2021, the group size had more than tripled. Michelle said "yes," and being very active on social media, she took to the role naturally. She helped answer questions and posted challenges to motivate members to try different workouts and push themselves.

It's easy to see why Michelle was plucked for the role. Her profile picture is of her in a tank top, drenched in sweat, copper-tinged brown locks framing her face with her eyes squinting, appearing to yell. Her expression reads, "I just crushed that workout; hear me roar!" Her posts are motivating, inspiring, and often funny. One day she posted a photo of herself doing the yoga pose called "crow." It involves squatting on the ground, placing your palms on the floor, and shifting your weight until you are balancing your knees on your elbows. In one photo she's balancing, and in the other she is splayed out on the floor. The accompanying post reads, "Sometimes you crow and sometimes you fall…either way, you keep at it! It is a metaphor for life!"[59]

Being a group moderator is a lot of work. She explained, "I won't even lie, it's a full-time job that we do not get paid for, but we all legitimately just love it. We just believe in the camaraderie of Black women. We believe in women wanting to better themselves. We believe in a safe space for women to vent and share frustrations."

The health and fitness-related posts in the group include everything from recommendations for the best stretch mark creams, protective hairstyles that can survive the daily sweat, recommendations for juicers, reducing new rider butt pain, and how to get faster riding out of the saddle. While the moderators try their best to keep the conversation focused on fitness and regularly remove posts that violate group rules, I have seen posts to celebrate engagements and other life milestones, posts about the hotness of certain instructors, sex toy reviews, and humor like a meme of Bernie Sanders on the Peloton in his inauguration day mittens. Workout inspiration aside, I can always count on the group to give me a good belly laugh.

The posts that inspire Michelle the most are from women who are struggling. They post that they are having a terrible

---

59 Michelle Guobadia, "Sometimes you crow and sometimes you fall," Facebook, January 17, 2021.

day for whatever reason, and the responses come flooding in. Posts commonly receive hundreds of "likes" and responses within minutes. And because having a Peloton connects the members, in addition to offering words of encouragement, the other thing we offer is support through group exercise. When someone is having a hard time, Michelle loves responses like, "I'll meet you on the bike in ten minutes. We're gonna sweat this out. What's your favorite ride? Let's go do it!"

The BGM group is a virtuous cycle. When Michelle posts and people tell her she's motivating and inspiring them, it pushes her to work even harder. She shared, "I feel very accountable to the group. When I don't post, I get DMs. I feel the need to post about me going on vacation like, 'Hey, I'm going to Antarctica for seventeen days so I will not be posting.'" If she doesn't do that, people will try to hunt her down.

Michelle works out about two hours a day. She'll string a series of twenty to thirty minute rides together with arms, core, and strength training. As she approached her fortieth birthday, she proudly proclaimed, "I'm in the best condition of my life."

I am grateful to ride virtually side by side with Michelle and over eighteen thousand BGM members. Together, we are getting fit and cheering each other on in a space that is for us and by us.

THE ACHE FOR HOME

I have been educated in and worked at predominantly white institutions for most of my career. For most Black folks, that is an inevitability of attaining mainstream success. That can be exhausting. When institutions seek to improve, they often tap people of color to put in additional time and emotional labor to facilitate the discussions, committees, and working groups leading the change.

When I look back over my life, spaces created for and by people of color have provided respite from the pressures of being Black in America. The Gathering Spot has helped nurture me as an entrepreneur. BGM inspires me to challenge my body in new ways, and Starshine & Clay provides spiritual nourishment. I would not be who I am today without these safe spaces to just "be"—boldly, unapologetically, and without explanation.

It has not been physically or psychologically safe to be Black in America since this country was founded. I believe that change is coming, and it is possible but also slow. Until we get a world free of racism, race-based violence, discrimination, and microaggressions, I will continue to seek out safe spaces that are welcoming and affirm my Blackness.

QUESTIONS FOR REFLECTION

1. How do you define "safe space"?
2. In what places do you feel like you can completely be yourself?
3. What are some of your earliest memories of people and organizations that really affirmed you and encouraged your learning and curiosity?
4. Are there areas in your life that you can cultivate spaces for marginalized groups to build community? At work? On a college campus or elsewhere?
5. How do you maintain boundaries when others make you feel unsafe?

CHAPTER 6

FAMILY

"Each member of the family...making his own patchwork quilt of reality - collecting fragments of experience here, pieces of information there. From the tiny impressions gleaned from one another, they created a sense of belonging..."

—TONI MORRISON, *THE BLUEST EYE*

I was born on September 2, 1971 to James Eric Williams and Willette Marie Sanders.

I hit the parent jackpot.

My father was born in Gilmore, Arkansas in 1942 to Fred Williams and Beatrice White. The family moved to Chicago when my father was a baby. My dad was a born entrepreneur. He began his career at eight years old, selling candy at school before graduating to a paper route. He once delivered hundreds of papers in a snowstorm with the help of his father. From gas to cups to packaging, it seems like there isn't a thing he hasn't sold. After high school, my father went into the military. He became a sergeant at age twenty-one, which helped shape his character, grit, and role as a leader. He grew up to build a successful business in the auto industry in Detroit.

When James Eric Williams enters a room, you know it. His personality is warm and magnetic. When my friends meet him once, they continue to ask about him forever. When he laughs, his eyelids swallow his twinkling green eyes whole. He laughs generously, and his favorite thing to laugh at is himself.

My mother, Willette Marie Sanders, was born in Augusta, Georgia in 1944 to a schoolteacher, Wilhelmina Avery, and an entrepreneur and brick mason, Rufus Sanders. She went on to college at Fisk University, a historically Black college in Nashville, Tennessee. She spent an extra year in college studying art and ceramics. She often walked around campus in paint-splattered overalls even though dresses, heels, and pearls were more in vogue. That was how a young woman, especially a young Black woman, was supposed to dress in order to be "acceptable." At Fisk, she got the opportunity to study with the world-renowned artist David Driskell. She talked about him and the influence he had on her a lot when I was younger.

After college, my mother went to Chicago to visit one of her girlfriends and former college roommates, Leslie. One taste of Chicago was all she needed; she never looked back. Her most viable career options as a Black female college graduate in the segregated South were teacher or nurse. After a couple other jobs, she eventually chose teacher and became a very good one.

As a teacher, my mom was unique in how she used the arts and creativity in every class. She bound her students' poetry into books and sent them off to national poetry competitions.

Like my grandmother, my mother played the piano. She created elaborate performances for her students, complete with acting, singing, and choreography—with me sometimes helping her. She was an impeccable seamstress who made clothes I was proud to wear. At heart, my mother was a creative.

While growing up, I felt my personality was most like my dad. In other ways, particularly with my creative pursuits, I was like my mom. Only later in life did I realize how much of an entrepreneurial spirit I had and how much my father influenced me. I am both of them in equal measure.

My mother passed away in 2009. The idea that she is not here to see what I have made of myself over the past twelve years, including writing *The Joy of Thriving While Black*, is almost too painful to bear. She is still alive in my heart each and every day, whispering, "You can do it. Keep going and don't ever stop."

My parents, including my "Bonus Mom" Kathy, are my biggest cheerleaders. They wanted me to go as far in any direction I wanted to go in life, and they gave me everything they could to help me thrive.

COMING HOME TO FAMILY

In June 2007, I moved to Atlanta, Georgia from Washington, DC for the job of my dreams—founding director of Posse Atlanta, a national leadership development college access organization. I had spent the past five years working at a private grantmaking foundation and was excited to transition to my first nonprofit executive leadership role. The only people I knew in Atlanta were my cousin Kanika and her husband, Zeda, who lived in the suburbs right outside of the city. They graciously allowed me to live with them and their two toddlers until I bought my house a few months later.

Fast forward to March 2019 when I started hatching my plan to leave my nonprofit job and launch my coaching business. I was thinking of all the ways I could lower my overhead and minimize financial risk. I texted Kanika and said, "Hey, if I decide to do this, can I stay with you for a little while until I transition?" In typical Kanika fashion, she texted me right back two words, "Come on."

By then, Kanika and Zeda had five amazing children, Sarah, Joshua, Bryson, Danyelle, and Austin. They ranged in age from four to sixteen and are the sweetest, smartest, and most loving kids you'd ever meet. When I first moved in, Joshua, the oldest boy, was my helper. He was so attentive, helping me move boxes and rearrange the furniture in my room. Every few days, he popped in and asked me if I needed help with anything. For Christmas, he gave me a book called *Toward a Meaningful Life* by Simon Jacobson, along with a beautiful letter that made connections between my work and the work of the author. You never know what teenagers are paying attention to. It was one of the most meaningful gifts I have ever received.

We had an incredible time. We played games, took photos and videos, and laughed and joked. We had movie nights, did Karaoke, had "one song" dance parties, painted, and built Legos. It was the most fun and active home life I have ever experienced.

Living with family was an adjustment and very different from growing up as an only child living alone most of my adult life. While there were times when the house was filled with the sounds that families make, I learned to take meetings in my closet if I needed to and even led and recorded guided meditations there. Over time, I could work, relax, and sleep with a lot more noise than I was used to. That served me well when I eventually moved into an apartment later in 2020.

I really enjoyed doing yoga and meditation with my youngest cousins. Bryson and Austin, ages seven and four, really got into it and asked to practice with me often. They could sit still with their eyes closed for up to three minutes, which was really impressive. Danyelle, who is six years old, is very high-energy, athletic, and a dancer. She didn't enjoy meditating as much. However, just when I thought "relaxation" wasn't Danyelle's thing, she came into my room one day to draw at my desk. Unsolicited, she asked, "Will you play the calm music?"

Bryson regularly asked me deep, thought-provoking questions. He was very curious about the plant in my bedroom. He loved watching new leaves open and wanted to know if the plant could feel his touch. Austin is the self-possessed, strong-willed one. One day I asked him to do something, and he said, "This is not your house, and I am the boss of my own body!" Those were facts. He often cracked me up with his defiance but also warmed my heart with his hugs.

Among the highlights of the summer of 2020 was getting to know my cousin Sarah better. She is the eldest and rising high school senior. When I started writing *The Joy of Thriving While Black,* I asked if she wanted to help by doing some research, and she eagerly agreed. It was a win-win situation because I needed the help, wanted someone else to talk to about the book, and the pandemic had derailed some of her other plans. Her work over the summer resulted in the research and summary of 228 online articles about topics including health disparities, education, history, and criminal justice. We met every Sunday; she was always prompt, well-prepared, and had thought-provoking commentary about what she was discovering.

Near the end of the summer, I asked Sarah if she wanted to write a paper to reflect on her experience. She eagerly said, "Yes!" Not many high school students raise their hand to write a paper during the summer. I was blown away by what I received, both the content and quality of the writing. She opened her paper with this, "What does it mean to be Black? I've never really asked myself that question, but over the past few months, we've seen disturbing answers to that question. To be unequal, to be in pain, to be ignored, to be vilified, to be 'thugs,' to be less than, unworthy, invisible. But at the same time, we've seen that to be Black is to be beautiful and resilient." After describing what she learned from her research, she ended with, "I've recently read the first chapter of the book, and seeing what lots of hard work, interviews, and ideas have manifested into was such a satisfying experience. From the first two interviews, I've already internalized bits of positivity that I'll carry for a long time…This whole experience has been an amazing, cool part of my summer that I didn't think would be too eventful."

Sarah is attending Georgia Tech University in the fall of 2021 on a full-tuition scholarship, and I could not be prouder.

By the end of my time there, I was completely in awe of Kanika. She and her husband are raising five children, and both work outside of the home. Kanika is a nurse at Grady Hospital in Atlanta and worked continuously throughout the pandemic. She also finds time to make her family delicious, healthy, home-cooked meals. She really listens to her children, cuddles them generously, and always makes time to create a teachable moment out of a mistake. She stays very calm in crisis, like the time Bryson poked himself in the eye with a stick and was screaming bloody murder. She is one of the most kind, patient, and nurturing people I have ever known.

When the coronavirus pandemic hit in February 2020, I was really grateful to still be living with family. Being bored or lonely was impossible. With eight people in a house, it is always a party.

Living with my family from July 2019 to September 2020 was a godsend. It gave me space to build a new business and a new life for myself as an entrepreneur. During two of my biggest career and life transitions, my family gave me a place to live filled with love. They allowed me to grow deeper roots as I got to know myself better and prepare for my next chapter.

RIDE OR DIE

"Majid is my biggest advocate, my biggest cheerleader. He knows me better than anybody." Already energetic and animated, when Adeola "Ola" Whitney talks about her husband, she lights up even more. I had always admired Ola's family dynamic and loved hearing stories about them when we worked together. We met at iMentor, a national nonprofit that builds mentoring relationships and empowers first-generation students to graduate high school and succeed in college.

Ola and her husband, Majid, an assistant vice president at Seton Hall University, are hard at work changing the world and raising three Black boys. The strength of their partnership is helping them achieve their professional goals, raise conscientious children, and enjoy life. They help each other thrive.

Being accountability partners on health and wellness goals is important to Ola and Majid. Ola explained that, together, they find ways "to center ourselves and our health." Health is an acute focus for them because they both lost their fathers young, at ages forty-nine and fifty-six. For Ola, the mission is simple: "We just want to live a long life."

Prior to the beginning of the pandemic, they used to work out together every morning and loved going on date nights. When the gyms shut down, they started walking six or seven days a week. One week they clocked in fifty miles. Their walks became their exercise and their dates, giving them time to talk, connect, and plan. They discussed everything from home renovations, the kids, and their careers.

When the pandemic began, Ola was a chief regional officer. During one of her walks with Majid, Ola decided to pursue a role as a chief executive officer. She wanted to continue to build on the legacy of activism and leadership passed down from her father.

When Ola was twelve years old, she went shopping with her parents in Columbus, Ohio, where she grew up. At the mall, they witnessed a very pregnant Black woman having an altercation with two white male security guards outside of JC Penney. Her family paused to observe, fearing the worst. Then it happened; the men shoved the woman to the ground.

Ola's father, Tajudeen, rushed over to intervene. As a result, the security guards called the police on him. The guards claimed the woman had stolen something from the store, which would never justify their actions. "What they didn't know," Ola explained, "was that my father was the editor of the only Black newspaper in Columbus. They put the whole story on the front page of the newspaper." She remembered taking the newspaper to school, showing it to her teacher and classmates saying, "This is about my dad. My dad did this." The story and resulting investigation led the NAACP to boycott JC Penney for an entire year. Ola was so proud.

Ola reflected, "It is interesting how something can have such an impact on your life, and it's come full circle for me." Ola traces much of her professional trajectory to this incident—becoming an African American studies major in college, going into the nonprofit sector, tutoring and mentoring students, and then taking on the biggest professional challenge of her life as CEO of Reading Partners, a national children's literacy nonprofit.

Ola and Majid met at Oberlin College and have been married for fifteen years. This is her philosophy:

"You have to be each other's hype man and woman. If your person doesn't want you to reach your true dreams in life, while trying to figure out what they can do to make it happen, that's just not a marriage."

Can I just pause here and say "#relationshipgoals"?

"I don't know that I'd be where I am professionally if it weren't for Majid." She recalled many years ago him telling her that she was better than the role she was in. "You could do your boss's job," he said. She protested stubbornly until she realized he was right. "I feel like that happens a lot...like he sees things sometimes way before I do."

Because Ola and Majid are thriving, their children are too. They are all brilliant, thoughtful, and creative. Their oldest, Taj, was admitted to Syracuse University, and because of his grades and other accomplishments, will attend tuition free. In his last year of high school, he went from not understanding the point of protesting to co-leading the largest Black Lives Matter protest in the history of Montclair, New Jersey where they live.

When she talked to one of her boys about her search for a CEO role, they thought it only natural that she be "number one," the one in charge. When she texted Taj to tell him that she received an offer, he replied, "Yo, that's what up, Mom. Congratulations!" That response meant the world to her.

Ola was thriving. She described herself as being in a place where "all feels right. There's like a level of balance. And what is not in balance, I feel like I have the power to shift and bring it back into balance." Her family gives her the love, support, and perspective to do just that.

LIKE WATER FOR TULIPS

One Saturday in April 2020, my father called me, very distressed. His sixty-two-year-old brother, my uncle Darius, a long-time sanitation worker in Chicago, was becoming increasingly concerned about his health and safety during the coronavirus pandemic. He was worried about his rights as an employee, and his messages to my father sounded desperate.

My father reached out to me to share my uncle's concerns and discuss his rights as a worker. We called my uncle together. During the call, my uncle shared that employees didn't have enough personal protective equipment, still had several men in one truck, and were not socially distancing. The call began as a strategy session about how he could advocate for himself and bring more attention to the plight of essential workers. The conversation evolved into us just catching up, laughing, and joking. He eventually did gain media attention for the working conditions and they slowly improved.

During the conversation, we relived one of my favorite family stories. In high school, Uncle Darius became obsessed with playing the piano. He would stand looking in the mirror for hours, pretending to play. Everyone thought it was funny, but he was very serious. My grandmother, B.B., eventually took him to his first piano lesson on November 4, 1976. It came as no surprise to him that he was an instant prodigy. After about a month, the teacher asked him if he was practicing at home. He wasn't because he didn't have a piano. That's when his big brother, my father, got together with B.B. to purchase one for him. The rest is history.

While the conversation began with a crisis, in the end, my uncle just needed someone to listen and empathize with what he was going through.

As a coach, I have experienced this dynamic repeatedly. I have had clients break down crying in the first session because they feel relieved just to have someone to talk to. The fact is, most people don't have someone who will listen without judgment or immediately get into "fix it" mode, offering unsolicited advice. My favorite quote about what we need instead is from sociologist Parker Palmer:

"The human soul doesn't want to be advised or fixed or saved. It simply wants to be witnessed—to be seen, heard, and companioned exactly as it is. When we make that kind of deep bow to the soul of a suffering person, our respect reinforces the soul's healing resources, the only resources that can help the sufferer make it through."[60]

I strive to embody this beautiful idea in my relationships and my coaching practice. I was grateful that my father and I could provide this to my uncle.

---

60 Parker J. Palmer, "The Gift of Presence, the Perils of Advice," *The On Being Project*, April 27, 2016.

The conversation with my uncle gave me and my father the idea to have weekly Zoom check-ins with the family. Every week, family members, both blood and chosen, called in from Atlanta, Chicago, Baltimore, and the suburbs of Detroit. It was the Williams and Butler families. My uncle Mitchell Butler and my father had been best friends for fifty-two years and our families were forever united.

We talked about all kinds of things on our calls, and the mood often reflected what was happening in the world.

Most weeks, our calls were lively, informative, and brought us closer together. We shared stories and memories and sometimes laughed until we cried. At the lowest point, our conversations mirrored the monotony of the pandemic. We circled the same two topics repeatedly. The first was our frustration with people not taking the mask mandate and social distancing seriously. The second was anger at the latest ridiculous thing President Donald Trump said or did. Those calls brought me down and made me wonder if they had run their course.

One week, my cousin Jenene asked if she could pose a question to help us get to know one another better. It was brilliant because it provided just the right amount of structure and focus to get everyone into the conversation. The first week, the question was about our favorite movie—the answers ranged from *The Godfather* to *The Wiz*. Another week, we shared favorite memories from our youth. One of my favorite stories, hands down, was from my cousin Derrick. His high school sweetheart worked at Popeye's, a fast-food chicken joint. When she got into the car after work, she smelled of chicken. When he told us that, he closed his eyes, smiled from ear to ear, and held an expression of bliss. To this day, for him, love smells like chicken.

One week we shared stories about our grandparents. My father, the only child of my grandparents on the call, had most of the juicy stories. He shared that my grandmother had been married twice before my grandfather and that he had been married three times before. Our collective reaction was worthy of a scene in a Spike Lee movie. Eyes bugged out, mouths gaped open, and hands flew up. Some folks fell out of view of the camera for a moment, trying to collect themselves.

My father also told a story about my paternal grandmother, Beatrice, also known as B.B., taking her first plane ride ever for my parents' wedding in Augusta, Georgia. Seeing her luggage outside the plane window distressed her; she didn't realize that they were putting it under the plane. On one of those calls, I learned that my cousin Debbie had a sister, Donna, who was born before her but passed away as a baby. She was the first grandchild, and her passing broke B.B.'s heart. I was also reminded that my cousin Jenene, like me, has a sibling in Germany, born when our fathers were in the military. By the time we got to the end of the hour and a half, someone said that the conversation should have been called "revelations."

Some moments on our calls were extremely moving. One week, my cousin, a police officer in Chicago, shared what it was like to be on duty during the racial justice protests of 2020. He was stationed at police headquarters on Michigan Avenue and then had to go protect property after it was destroyed. He said that doing his job during the protests was like trying to work "while a bunch of your angry cousins yelled at you." He also confirmed what we heard on the news about white agitators, wearing all black, who hung out in the back of the crowd instigating conflict. It was impossible to tell who a sincere protester was and who was there just to cause trouble.

The whole situation made his young daughter afraid and anxious. She supported and empathized with peaceful protesters but was also worried for her father's safety. He talked to us about what he was going through for about twenty minutes and cried the entire time. I had not really thought about what it was like to be a Black police officer in that climate, working long hours under really difficult circumstances. At a time when people were circulating articles saying, "Check on your Black friends and coworkers," his response was, "No one is checking on us." It was devastating.

Our conversations became much more upbeat at the end of Donald Trump's presidency. In January 2021, we talked about our hopes for the new administration led by President Joseph Biden and Vice President Kamala Harris. We covered everything from federal coordination to improve distribution of the COVID-19 vaccine, appointing new Supreme Court justices, and legalizing marijuana. One thing was high on all of our lists. We wanted justice to be delivered swiftly to the insurrectionists who stormed the US Capitol on January 6, 2021. In their attempt to disrupt the counting of electoral ballots to certify President Joe Biden's victory, five people were killed and 140 were injured.[61]

One Saturday, my aunt Yvonne told a beautiful story about a bunch of tulips she bought. She didn't put enough water in the vase, the tulips quickly absorbed it all, and before she knew it, they were completely flopped over. Ignoring her

---

61   Eric Levenson, Amir Vera and Mallika Kallingal, "What We Know about the 5 Deaths in the Pro-trump Mob That Stormed the Capitol," *CNN*, January 8, 2021.

first instinct to throw them away, she filled the vase up with water and went upstairs to get dressed for the day. An hour and a half later when she returned downstairs, the tulips were upright again, perky and plump.

Yvonne is a public school administrator who helped with crisis management. One day, one of the bus drivers dropped a child off at the wrong day care center after school. The principal from the child's school got in serious trouble. When Yvonne met with the principal, she was so distraught she thought she would never recover. The tulips popped into Yvonne's mind. She told the woman, "No, we're going to support you, pour into you, and prop you up and just like those tulips. We're going to get you back on your feet." Hearing that story just melted our hearts, and we all expressed gratitude to Yvonne for sharing it.

One thing we could all agree on was that our weekly calls were like a refuge. Just when it felt like the walls were closing in, we knew we would be together again. Our calls became a container to hold our deepest fears and biggest dreams that included some day having a family compound. I cherished those calls. In getting to know my family better, I grew to know myself better. They lifted my spirits, kept me well-informed, and inevitably, produced some of the heartiest laughs I experienced the entire time we were on lockdown. Those consistent calls kept me going from week to week. They were like water for tulips.

TO THEM I BELONG

The stories in this chapter represent moments in time in our families, but families can be as complex and broken as they are beautiful. Families are often the first places where we learn about the world and our place in it. Some of what we learn helps us thrive. Other things we want to let go.

We get to choose. We also get to choose family the way my father and Uncle Mitch chose each other fifty-two years ago and the way Ola and Majid chose each other. Whether blood or chosen, we belong to our families.

QUESTIONS FOR REFLECTION

1. How would you describe your family to someone who has never met them before?
2. How are you like your family? How are you different?
3. What family stories informed your view of the world? Which do you want to keep? Which do you want to release?
4. What kind of role model do you want to be to people in your family?
5. Who is your chosen family?

PART III

"I thought I told you that we won't stop."

—MULTIPLE ARTISTS

CHAPTER 7

RESILIENCE

"Grief and resilience live together."

— MICHELLE OBAMA, *BECOMING*

In 2017, I experienced a series of trying events that almost broke me. Instead, they helped me get even stronger, reshaping how I thought about my life and career.

Learning to pick ourselves up repeatedly, becoming wiser along the way, is key to thriving. This quality, also known as "resilience," can be simply defined as "capacity to recover from difficult life events."[62] Beyond resilience, there is also post-traumatic growth, which is "positive change experienced as a result of the struggle with a major life crisis or a traumatic event."[63] Being resilient doesn't mean that you don't experience pain, sadness, and grief. In fact, resilient

---

62 Katie Hurley, "What Is Resilience? Your Guide to Facing Life's Challenges, Adversities, and Crises," *Everyday Health*, December 10, 2020.

63 "What is PTG?" University of North Carolina Charlotte, accessed February 1, 2021.

people are great at working through the emotions that accompany challenging times.

Aside from a few brief periods, I was physically active my entire life. As a child, I loved physical education class and spent my entire recess time on the playground running or jumping double dutch. I was down for dodgeball, kickball, and even flag football. I was "that girl." In my lifetime, I have been a dancer and practiced the Afro-Brazilian martial art capoeira. I have run dozens of 5Ks, 10Ks, and one half marathon, which is 13.1 miles. I am also a yoga instructor who practices yoga regularly. Moving my body makes me feel strong and brings me joy.

My lifetime of movement was profoundly disrupted on Labor Day weekend, 2017. It was my forty-sixth birthday celebration, and it was epic. I partied for four days with the gusto of a twenty-five-year-old. I taught three yoga classes, had a birthday brunch in the park with my friends, went to a jazz concert, and danced all day at Atlanta's legendary House in the Park music festival. After that, I decided to do some capoeira and top it off with two turns of double dutch.

I was in my flow...jumping, crisscrossing, one leg, two legs, faster and faster, hopping in circles like I was back on my elementary school playground. Jumping double dutch was coming back to me like riding a bike, and it was exhilarating!

After my first turn, I felt like I was just warming up, so I begged for another. Just as I was getting into the flow again, I heard a pop and felt a searing pain. I looked around in shock and confusion. I thought I had been hit in the heel by the rope, but it had never felt like that before.

I tried to take a step, but I collapsed in pain. Fortunately, I had friends around who could support me as I hopped my way to the car. When I got home, I realized I had ruptured my

Achilles tendon. There was a huge space where that strong, tight tendon was supposed to be connected, and I could not move my foot. My doctors confirmed my self-diagnosis with an MRI, and I was scheduled for surgery on my ruptured tendon three days later.

Achilles tendon surgery is extremely painful and invasive. One day, I was researching the recovery process and accidentally encountered a photo of the surgery. I almost fainted.

My pain level after surgery was high, or so I thought. But when the nerve block they injected me with before surgery wore off, the pain was an eleven on a scale from one to ten. The pain killers were effective for four out of the five hours between doses, but then the pain would creep back in. I would spend the last excruciatingly long hour watching the clock. I began taking the meds slightly closer together every time. It was my first time ever on painkillers, and I could see how easily a person could slip into addiction if they had to endure pain like that for months or years. I vowed to myself that I wouldn't refill the prescription, and I didn't.

At the time of my accident, I had a very intense job that required travel. I love traveling, even for work, so I was happy when I was well enough to get back to it. About six weeks after surgery, I hopped back on a plane for a business trip. And when I say "hopped," I really mean placing my right knee on a scooter with my foot in a boot and pushing my way around with my left leg. I got good at it, and despite the reasons for being on a knee scooter, it was sometimes a fun way to get around.

My first trip was to Detroit. By then, I had learned to navigate streets and sidewalks and Ubers, so I felt confident. The morning after I arrived in town, I was scooting myself toward the shower when my scooter caught the edge of the rug.

I started falling toward my injured foot (that was unbooted because I was getting in the shower), and out of instinct, I put my foot down on the floor to brace my fall.

The pain I experienced was ten times worse than rupturing the tendon. The impact of my foot on the ground reopened the four-inch incision running up my tendon, and it started bleeding profusely. And when I say "profusely," I mean like blood in a Quentin Tarantino movie. I sobbed and wailed like a simultaneously sad and angry toddler as I used everything within reach to stop the bleeding. When I finally got it together, I called my cousin Kanika to see if I could get away with not going to the emergency room. That was the last place I wanted to go in Detroit. Her advice was that if I couldn't put the entire tip of a Q-Tip into the wound, I could probably get by. That was all that I needed to hear. I bandaged myself up using whatever they had in the hotel first aid kit and took the first thing smoking back to Atlanta.

This incident was a big setback to my healing from the surgery. Before my second accident, I was right on the verge of being able to walk in my boot. Instead, I had to get my incision closed and wait for it to heal again before beginning to walk.

By then, I was going into my third month of recovery. For three months, I didn't walk, drive, travel, or go up and down the stairs of my home. I had to shower on a bench with a tight cast cover to keep my incision from getting wet and infected. I was beginning to feel claustrophobic in my own body and started having phobias of falling, car accidents, and bad dreams about other calamities. I was having violent muscle spasms in my injured leg at night, which was, according to my doctor, the nerves in my calf relearning how to connect with my heel. The sensation caused me to kick my leg, which would jerk me awake, heart racing and in pain. If it wasn't so painful, it would almost be comical. Needless to say, I wasn't getting quality sleep.

One thing the doctors told me to look out for was blood clots, which can form in the lower leg after surgery. One day I felt a little pain in my calf. Being hypervigilant as I am about these things, I went to the doctor for an ultrasound. Sure enough, I had a blood clot. That meant extended travel restriction, injecting myself in the stomach with blood thinners twice daily, and having my blood drawn every few days to regulate my blood thinner medication. My hemoglobin count and blood pressure were also low, so my doctor told me to take iron and vitamin D.

At four months, I finally started walking and physical therapy, which was great progress. But I had developed a very thick keloid scar that had to be manipulated and scraped by my physical therapist to soften it and increase my range of motion. That process was so excruciating that I often cried during the sessions. I went through this three days a week, leaving the PT office nauseous and with a headache. It was hell.

Physical therapy was helping, but I felt impatient. My surgeon wanted me to work on doing single-leg calf raises, and when I tried, I just felt intense pain in my Achilles. My calf muscle was not responding at all. For weeks, I tried with all my might without producing even a millimeter lift.

As time passed, I felt my energy depleting and my mood worsening. I ignored it at first, figuring that my body and mind were just adjusting to all that I was going through physically. My doctors reassured me that my fatigue indicated my body's need for more rest to heal from what was a more traumatic injury than I ever realized. While all of that was true, I was also slipping into a depression.

It didn't help that I was falling further and further behind at work, was not hitting my milestones, and was stressed beyond measure. It was honestly the first time in my career that I felt so behind for so long and couldn't find the solutions and support I needed to push through.

I cycled through depression and anxiety until I felt myself moving toward panic. One day, my level of anxiety frightened me. By then, I could drive, so I decided to drive myself to advanced care. I was driving down the highway in the right lane, trying to be calm and honor the speed limit, even though I never wanted to get anywhere faster in my life. My anxiety level was so high I thought I was on the verge of a panic attack. Then I started panicking that I was driving while panicking. When I got to my doctor's office, my blood pressure was so high that the nurse told me they would have to admit me to the hospital if it did not come down quickly. I did some deep breathing, meditated, and brought my blood pressure down significantly, which was good. Seeing the measurable impact of meditation on my body was also cool.

Lying there in advanced care, I realized that something had to give. I was completely burnt out.

I had been talking to my boss, Ola, about how I was feeling, and she was very supportive but also not quite sure what to do. She had already touched base with HR about options. Our last conversation was on a Friday before she was leaving the country for vacation. She told me to talk to the HR department, let them know how much time I needed, and that she had already approved it. I was so relieved.

I took a one-month leave of absence from work. Although my boss and organization handled it superbly and supported me 100 percent, that time off was one of the most terrifying professional and personal decisions I have ever made. I was really worried about what people would think and how things would be when I returned.

During that month, I was hyper-motivated to do all I could to recover: yoga, meditation, extra physical therapy, quality time with friends, therapy, journaling, and above all, rest. I started to really reflect on my job and what I wanted to do with my life. I dug deep into the question, "How can I best use my talents, passions, experience, and education for the benefit of others?" The answer had been bubbling beneath the service for about a decade. I wanted to become a full-time coach.

I returned to my job feeling healthier, refreshed, and more focused. I also achieved the goal I had been working toward: launching a new program site in Baltimore. That victory gave me the confidence to start planning my exit. A little over a year later in June 2019, I began coach training, and in January 2020, I launched my full-time practice.

I am not happy that I ruptured my Achilles tendon, got burnt out, and had to take time off work. However, my ability to adapt and create meaning from that experience has been transformative. It allowed me to build resilience and gave me a powerful story to tell.

As a coach, my story is one of the most vital tools in my toolkit. It deepens my well of compassion and empathy and helps other people with similar experiences, including burnout, connect with me. My experience sparked a chain of events that gave me the courage to pursue my dream career, one that I am thriving in.

AIN'T NO MOUNTAIN HIGH ENOUGH

Exhausted and facing a steep hill near the end of her first marathon, Angie cranked up her music and danced her way up.

That is Angie O'Neal.

Angie was diagnosed with breast cancer in 2006. She was devastated, but not so much by the thoughts of her own mortality. As a wife, worker, and mother of three, Angie thought about her responsibilities and all the things she had to manage. It caused her a lot of anxiety and guilt.

Fortunately, Angie's cancer treatment was successful, and the experience had a powerful impact on her. "It almost shocked me into learning that I could have kind of a new lease on life," she said. "I could stop feeling guilty about any and everything. It gave me the freedom to say, you gotta live your life; you gotta try new things and stop being so scared."

It took a little time, but after undergoing cancer treatment, Angie slowly began working out again. One day she was at her gym, which had exactly three pieces of cardio equipment: an elliptical machine, a stationary bike, and a treadmill. Until that day, she had avoided the treadmill like the plague. But having completed her other training, she gave in and hopped on because the elliptical and bike were occupied. The run hurt—a lot. But when she was done, she felt her heart pumping, her blood was circulating, and she felt great.

This was around 2008, right before my friend Indra and I founded Urban Run Club in Atlanta. I was new to running, had completed a couple of 5Ks, and needed the support and accountability of a group. Indra, an avid runner, was our leader, and Angie was one of the first people to join the group. Angie reminded me that she ran her first 10K because of me. I had asked a few friends to run with me to raise money for cancer research. The cause resonated because my mother died from lung cancer, and of course, the cause was also close to Angie's heart.

Over the years, Angie continued to run and left me in the dust soon after she really dedicated herself to it.

Bad news came again for Angie in 2016. Her cancer had returned. While she had a decent prognosis, she faced much more invasive surgery before undergoing chemo. While she was shocked that her cancer came back, she told me she jumped into it with a different mindset. She decided, "I'm just gonna keep doing everything that I can possibly do while going through the treatment. Every single day that I'm here on this earth, I have to fight to stay alive." Angie had chemotherapy every other week. In the weeks between, she got friends together for happy hours. It was amazing to see her tackle the experience with such a commitment to still enjoying her life.

Several years before her first cancer diagnosis, Angie had heard about people running marathons which are 26.1 miles. She thought they were crazy. Then she heard about a man who had survived lung cancer and had run a marathon around the time that Oprah Winfrey did it in 1994. She can remember thinking to herself, "Oh my God, anything is possible."

At age forty-five, Angie decided that she would run a marathon when she was fifty, which gave her ample time to get mentally prepared and train. But when her cancer came back at the age of forty-seven, that's when it hit her, "Oh, wait a second. If you don't do this now, you might not ever have the opportunity to do it." Before she even completed her chemo treatments, she signed up for a marathon. "I knew that was crazy. I thought, *We're just gonna see where this takes me.* It was a journey; it was another thing that I needed to accomplish in my life. Ultimately, that probably helped me get through the chemo and everything because I had another focus."

On race day, March 19, 2017, Angie arrived at the starting line hyped. As she joined the sea of ten thousand-plus runners who were also running the Publix Marathon in Atlanta, she felt ready and supported. A friend of hers had organized a large group of Black folks to run the race, and people showed up in record numbers. A fraction of marathoners is Black, so for Angie and all her friends, just being there was extremely significant.

She started the race strong, but consistent with her past races, maybe a little too fast. At the halfway mark thirteen miles in, she realized that her pace wasn't sustainable. She was also frustrated with her playlist, which just wasn't working for her anymore. She could no longer see her friends, so she started to feel alone. Angie took a deep breath, adjusted her music, and began what she described as a brand-new race.

At that point, she wasn't feeling nearly as good as when she started, and that's when the steep Atlanta hills appeared. Passing people cheering and waving and having a great time gave her a little boost, but just past that, she was starting to "lose it." That's when she decided to pause to give herself a little pep talk. "It's okay, Angie. You are still here."

Angie began slowly up the hills and started to see runners she recognized again. She said to herself, "Let me at least just catch up with them. If I catch up with them, I'll still feel like I'm in this race." She doesn't know if they slowed down for her, but she caught up, and together they tackled the hills one by one. As they approached another hill, she saw two other friends who joined the pack. They stayed together and passed the twenty-mile mark without Angie even realizing they'd passed it.

By then, the group's bond was solidified. As a team of five, they would get through the race together. If someone started walking, no one left; they just walked up the hill together. If someone lagged, everyone waited.

Angie felt mentally strong until she approached a hill that she knew would be tough. She told me, "In my mind, I'm thinking, *I don't think I'm gonna be able to do it. Twelfth Street is a beast, and it's gonna kill me. I don't want to completely die on it.* And then a good song came on. I can't remember what song it was, but I loved it." So, what did she do? She cranked up the music and danced up the hill.

"Somebody was taking pictures of me because I'm just high-fiving people and pretending like I'm feeling great, and all that. But I was just in my head, and I was just listening to the music, and I just danced," she recounted. Somebody posted a picture of it later and one of the comments was, "Is Angie dancing?"

As Angie approached the last mile, she saw her daughter Joa, who joined her in the run to the finish. Somehow, she found a fifth gear, and she and her crew crossed the finish line quickly. When she burst into tears, she was completely surprised by the emotion that overcame her. Sometimes alone, but mostly with her squad and ultimately her family, she had walked, run, and danced her way to the finish. Angie was a marathoner.

Marathons are such powerful metaphors for resilience. Even though I have only run a half marathon, I could relate to the ebbs and flows of Angie's journey. From mile to mile, your emotions shift from exuberance to dread, to hope, then despair, and back again. However, if you keep putting one foot in front of the other, you will reach the end and feel stronger for it. I am one of many people who admires Angie for her determination to complete this feat not long after cancer treatment.

A little over three years later, Angie is happy, healthy, and, at age fifty-two, stronger than ever. She still runs, lifts weights, bikes long distances, and has recently started creating these crazy, insane workout videos with two of her daughters who are in their twenties. When I asked what working out meant to her, she said, "It almost means everything to me...survival, strength, power. Being a mom and even with my job, trying to succeed...I don't feel like I can do any of those things unless I feel strong." Moving her body is key to her resilience and ability to thrive.

WE BEND, BUT WE DO NOT BREAK

There is no life without pain, loss, sickness, and grief. However, without those human experiences, we could not have strength and resilience.

The entire Black American experience is a story of resilience. The fact that we are even here is a testament to our ancestors' resilience. We can be powerfully motivated by the struggles of those who came before us. When we continue to bounce back every time we are knocked down, we also model that for those who will come after us. Thriving is not only our birthright, but our obligation.

QUESTIONS FOR REFLECTION

1. How do you define "resilience"?
2. What have you overcome that makes you feel stronger and wiser?

3. What resources can you draw on to help you overcome obstacles? Friends? Family? Therapy?
4. Are you plagued with negative feelings about your past? How might you reframe those stories to remind you of how much you've learned and how resilient you are?
5. Think of something scary you want to accomplish. How might doing it make you more powerful when it's done?

CHAPTER 8

SELF-CARE

"A violinist had a violin, a painter his palette. All I had was myself. I was the instrument that I must care for."

—JOSEPHINE BAKER

"You have the right to change your mind." I can remember the first time that sentence struck me as being so potent. It communicated that I had the right to do what was best for me, even if it meant backing out of a previous commitment. For me, this is as critical to self-care as spa days, pedicures, and journaling. Self-care isn't just an appointment on the calendar, but also taking good care of yourself, mind, body, and spirit, day in and day out.

In the summer of 2019, I reconnected with a former non-profit colleague while doing some work at The Gathering Spot. As we caught up about our lives and work, it turned out that much of what we were doing professionally was aligned. After many conversations over several months, he hired me to design and deliver a training for his nonprofit. It was my biggest contract to date, and I was thrilled. Our work was to begin in May 2020 and end in August.

Our work together landed in the middle of the racial justice protests of 2020. These events were happening in the pressure cooker of the Trump administration, the restlessness caused by the pandemic and the ongoing need to self-quarantine.

On June 5, I led a free, guided community meditation over Zoom, which I called "A Deep Breath for Black Lives." Fifty people showed up. At the end of the meditation, I posed the following questions and provided the opportunity for reflection and journaling:

- How can I use my power, position, or privilege to support those who have less of it than I do?
- How can I be a greater advocate for justice?
- What action can I take when no one is watching, there are no pats on the back and no social media "likes"?
- How can I be more peaceful?
- Who can I turn to for support?
- What do I need to do to take really good care of myself?

These were all questions that I was grappling with.

The next day I was to lead my first training for my new nonprofit client. I, as a Black woman, was set to face a Zoom room full of people to train them for a well-meaning, white-led organization that had no racial justice frame to their work. That fact had bothered me from the beginning, but suddenly, the need to represent the organization publicly brought it to a head. I suggested that the leadership write a statement addressing their stance on racial justice. They did that, but it was narrowly focused on the protests. When the protests died down a few weeks later, the statement didn't feel as relevant, so I made some suggestions for updating it. That was not the work I had signed up for, but it felt important. However, I knew I was sliding down a slippery slope.

The racial justice context aside, the engagement had already been challenging. The nonprofit was a brand-new organization experiencing the growing pains of any start-up. So, in creating the training, I was actually helping them figure out a lot about their organization and philosophy. Our planning meetings always went over time and became increasingly tense. I facilitated the two-part, three-hour sessions about a half dozen times, and the client made changes to the order and the content every single time. This resulted in me having to change the entire script of each three-hour training and adjust the timestamps for each slide. It was maddening.

Nothing the client did was horrible, but the times we were living in tried my patience. Working while Black in the summer of 2020 was hard. I was tired of hearing about the killings of Black people and was tired of having to shield my eyes every time a video popped up on my screen documenting one of them. Black death and trauma were on a continuous loop.

I was tired of the Band-Aid solutions to systemic problems fueled by racism. I was tired of explaining. After two decades in the nonprofit sector, I was tired of having the same conversations repeatedly with white people. I was tired of the performative allyship. I was tired of walking the tightrope of sharing what I thought while also not showing up as the "angry Black woman."

I felt like I had to navigate racism, my feelings about current events, educate people about what was going on and how I was feeling, all while helping well-meaning white folks become better allies.

A widely circulated article by Danielle Cadet captured my feelings so well. In it, she described a tale of two pandemics:

"Over the last few months, Black people have not only watched their friends and family members die at higher rates from the coronavirus, but they have also watched people who look like them be gunned down while going for a jog, be murdered in their homes, threatened while bird watching in Central Park, and mercilessly choked on camera. And every day, we have woken up and answered the emails and gotten on the Zoom calls. We've showed up with a smile and put the pain and fear behind us. We've swallowed the rage...."[64]

By that point, I was choking on rage, frustration, and grief. Hearing the "shock" and "outrage" of some white folks along with "this is not what America is" just infuriated me even more. Were we living in the same country?

I was a consultant, not a member of the nonprofit's staff, but I felt myself getting sucked deeper and deeper into their work. Let's be clear. I let it happen. I cared about doing right by the client, their trainees, and ultimately, the people they served. Every time I relaxed the boundaries I had set, I convinced myself it was for a good reason.

I was very thoughtful about the language we used and often cringed when I heard phrases like "these people," or questions about whether poor people even had goals. I worked hard to ensure that our training materials didn't

---

64 Danielle Cadet, "Your Black Colleagues May Look like They're Okay — Chances Are They're Not," *Refinery 29*, May 28, 2020.

reinforce stereotypes about Black folks or the poor. That sometimes required reframing some of the work they had done before I came on board.

Our conversations about racism and racial justice got hotter and hotter every time I talked to my client; it was just a matter of time before they boiled over. Then the articles started circulating. Despite my request not to be included in staff emails, I kept receiving articles they were sharing to educate themselves on race and racism. It was just too much.

Meanwhile, the trainings were running behind schedule, and they wanted to extend our contract until October. At first, I agreed. Then I changed my mind. I ended the agreement and walked away from a couple thousand dollars. Choosing to step away was a radical act of self-care, and it was so freeing. It ended the dread I was starting to feel whenever I engaged with the client. I became more relaxed and had more space to tend to myself during a very tumultuous time.

We often talk about self-care as if it is synonymous with "pampering." It is bigger than that. Self-care is an extension of self-love. It means doing what you need to do for you, even if it is uncomfortable or inconvenient for other people. According to an article by Dr. Shainna Ali in *Psychology Today*, "Self-love is an active, engaged process that evokes a wealth of positive benefits. A critical component in self-love is recognizing your limits, needs, and worth, and asserting intrapersonal and interpersonal boundaries as needed to uphold them."[65]

I learned so much from that experience, including how to set better boundaries with clients and how to manage my emotional energy. The experience also helped clarify what

---

65   Shainna Ali, "What Self-Love Isn't," *Psychology Today*, February 5th, 2019.

kind of work I wanted to do. It was a lot to navigate as a new business owner, but I've learned that I can never go wrong when I trust my instincts and honor what I need.

YOU HAVE TO CURATE YOUR LIFE

Beatrice Dixon is the CEO of the multimillion-dollar The Honey Pot Company, which she founded in 2014. I met her through our mutual friend, Indra, back when they both worked for Whole Foods. Beatrice founded The Honey Pot Company after curing herself from a long bout of bacterial vaginosis. She founded the clean, plant-based feminine care company to share what she learned with others.

Leading a company throughout 2020 was challenging, especially on the supply chain management front, but Bea took it in stride. As she explained, "Illnesses happen. Death happens. The economy drying up happens. These things just happen to be a part of life." The year 2020 gave Bea more time to lean into the life she wants to live and use every decision to curate it.

There was a time, however, that Bea struggled with that. One day she got into the car where her mother was waiting for her after a doctor's appointment. Her mother looked her in the eye and said, "You know you're going to die one day. Every moment that you're not living your absolute most beautiful life is a wasted moment." Whew! It takes a mama to cut to the heart of the matter like that. Bea's mother was speaking to the fact that Bea hadn't been well for a while. She wasn't happy. She was in a relationship that wasn't good for her, and she felt like she was walking on eggshells. As she put it, "I was in fight-or-flight mode, all the time." Her doctor confirmed what she already felt inside; her thyroid levels were off.

A couple of weeks after that, Bea started choosing her life.

The combination of her health scare and her mother's words lit a spark in her. Bea wanted a different life, so she started listening to her inner guidance more closely and started seeking. She read *The Four Agreements* by Don Miguel, and then she devoured *A Course in Meditation: A 21-Day Workout for Your Consciousness* by Osho. From there, she read *The Daily Stoic* and *The Secrets of the Golden Flower.* They were all books about the mind and the art of living. The more she continued to "chase her happiness," the more amazing resources she came across, which reminds me of one of my favorite quotes by the Sufi poet Rumi, "What you seek is seeking you."

Now, Bea is much more intentional about how she curates her life. It begins with her physical environment. She explained, "I need to see plants. I need the space to be clean, and I need it to smell good. When I walk into my closet, I need it to be organized."

From there, her self-care extends to her body. It is important to Bea to smell good and wear the clothes she loves and feels comfortable in. She is meticulous about the vitamins she takes. She eats a healthy, clean diet but is not rigid about it. This last point is critical. As she explained it, "I'm not gonna repress what I really want because that is where depression lives and anxiety comes from…also neurosis." While she eats a mostly plant-based diet, when she wants some Wagyu beef, she has it and enjoys every bite.

This point really resonated with me. Rigidity on the path to self-love, acceptance, and self-care is counterproductive. If we're constantly beating ourselves up because we aren't doing things perfectly, all we do is suffer. This is not caring for ourselves.

Beatrice is very clear about this point:

"I love humanity. I love my family. I love my friends. But nobody is more important than me."

To understand our needs, we have to get still and listen. Once we hear what we need to hear, then we must commit to curating the life that allows us to meet those needs.

YOU ARE WORTHY

I believe that at the heart of our willingness to commit to self-care is worthiness. Do we feel worthy of our own care, time, and attention? We need this not only so we can be well, but so we can be our best selves for our work, our friends, and our family.

India Arie is my worthiness guru. She is a singer, songwriter, and recording artist who has carried us on her journey to self-love through her art. I have practiced and taught yoga to her song "I Am Light" on many occasions. The song, both lullaby and mantra, is simple, sweet, and powerful, which is why her music resonates so much. Her song "Worthy" reminds her listener that she knows what we're going through because she's been there too. She also reminds us that we're all worthy of things like love, life, and saying "no" to the things that do not serve us. Arie is also a yogi and daily meditator. I kinda feel like we should be friends.

Arie learned these lessons the hard way. She worked in an industry that valued a beauty standard she doesn't reflect. An industry that she describes as being racist and sexist. While she had been nominated for twenty-three Grammys, she only won three. Before she began winning, the losses were crushing, and it didn't help that they were repeatedly reported as "snubs." Once she realized she was attaching too much of her self-worth to external validation, she began to heal. She also became an independent artist, doing her work on her own terms, surrounded by people who loved and supported her. She realized, "There is nothing wrong with me. I have to remind myself of that all the time. I've been through a lot of things and survived a lot of things that made me just feel flawed, wounded, and damaged."[66]

I could relate. In 2019, I participated in Octavia Raheem's HELD Mentorship program for yoga teachers and wellness professionals. In one of our retreats, we did a session to uncover our "personal lie." This lie is at the heart of all our negative self-talk. Our facilitator, Lorri Palko, asked a series of questions to which we responded over the course of an hour. Layer by layer, we peeled the onion. When we got to the end, my personal lie was, "There is something wrong with me." Uncovering that broke my heart, but as we shared around the circle, I realized that the exercise resonated with everyone. Shining the light on the darkness of our personal lie instantly weakened it and allowed us to uncover what was really true.

Afterward, we wrote a personal truth as an antidote to the lie. My truth was, "I am worthy because I exist." I wrote that truth in my journal every day for months, and it shifted something in me; it made me feel steadier.

I have found the feeling of unworthiness to be common among friends and clients, though we don't often name it that. We may experience it as guilt, feeling undeserving of things we have, especially if close friends and family are struggling. One of the most ubiquitous expressions of unworthiness I have seen is imposter syndrome, the feeling that we aren't smart enough or accomplished enough to be in our roles.

---

66   India Arie, "Worthy Q & A 1 of 2," June 4, 2018, in *Songversation*, podcast, 7:30.

The good news is once we are aware of feelings of unworthiness, we can unravel them to give ourselves the care we need and deserve.

YOU DON'T HAVE TO EARN YOUR POSITION IN THE WORLD

"Everything you do feels like *the biggest, most amazing thing you have ever done in your life!*" That is how Bassey Ikpi describes the feeling of having hypomania associated with bipolar II disorder in her book, *I'm Telling the Truth, but I'm Lying.*[67] She describes it like being on a Ferris wheel for the first time and "your entire body tingled with this intersection of joy and indestructibility and fearlessness and that good anxious recklessness." Having bipolar disorder has taught Bassey what it means to take really good care of herself.

I met Bassey, ex-poet, writer, and mental health advocate, when I was in law school at Northwestern. She was dating one of my classmates at the time. Our meeting was brief, but I got the opportunity to hear her read her poetry, and it was phenomenal.

Fast forward over twenty years, and I heard Bassey on *NPR* commenting on the way people talk about Kanye West and his sometimes-bizarre words and behavior. Because they share the experience of having bipolar disorder, she has a lot of empathy for him. What she shared in the interview was so striking: We do not have to like a person to have compassion for their mental health challenges. She also commented that Kanye West would not see or care about people's mean-spirited comments and social media posts about him. However,

---

67 Bassey Ikpi, *I'm Telling the Truth but I'm Lying* (New York: Harper Perennial, 2019), 143.

other people will. She explained, "All these people that you do have an impact on are seeing the way that you treat this person. And they're either going to hide from you, they're going to dismiss their own feelings, or they're going to feel as though they're not worthy of empathy and kindness and grace and forgiveness."[68]

As a society, our jokes, misconceptions, and myths about mental health are hurting people we don't even know are struggling. This is even worse in the Black community, where there can be distrust of and lack of access to mental health services.

On a whim, I reached out to interview Bassey after hearing the NPR interview. When she agreed, I was both thrilled and honored.

When I asked her about thriving, she described it as a relatively new idea for her because "the last five to fifteen years has been about just staying alive and doing enough to make sure that I showed up every day." As she continued to expand on her answer, she made the following statement with a strength and steadiness in her voice that matched her conviction. Thriving means "putting my mental wellness before anything or anybody."

For Bassey, caring for herself means creating structure. This is especially important for her because she has to manage her medication. She uses a wellness and meditation app and a productivity planner. She's learned to break things down into bite-sized pieces and give herself permission to fail. Releasing perfectionism has also been important to her;

68 Tonya Mosley and Allison Hagan, "'Mental Illness Is Not an Excuse, but It Is a Reason': How to Talk about Kanye West's Behavior," *WBUR,* June 29, 2020.

she used to put too much pressure on herself before she even started a project.

Bassey has been good at basically everything she has touched in her career, but she felt like she was always chasing happiness and success because, at her core, she didn't feel steady. She is in a different place now. "Right now, if nothing else changes for me—if I never get another job, if some of these other projects that I'm working on don't pan out, I'm still okay…happy where I am," she explained.

Bassey has come to terms with the simple fact that we can't count on being happy every day. Being human means living through a lot of ups and downs. As she described, "For someone who has bipolar disorder, I don't trust my emotions as it is."

Contentment is more reliable than happiness, and I think it is underrated. In a culture obsessed with striving, it can actually be a relief to just take a deep breath and be okay with where you are right now.

To prioritize her self-care, Bassey had to overcome the need to be "nice." For her, "nice" meant putting herself aside for other people. Instead, she wants to be "kind." The way she chooses "kind" over "nice" is by saying "no." Bassey has achieved a level of public success that leads to many requests, pressures, and expectations. Since releasing her book, there is already pressure to write another, but for now, she has decided that she does not enjoy writing for work. "I'm not going to do things because other people tell me that they like that I do that thing. What I have done I'm proud of. I don't feel any need to constantly prove that I deserve to be here, or I deserve to be loved and appreciated. I'm not trying to earn my position in the world anymore," she declared.

Saying "no" used to be more difficult for Bassey. Declining meant coming up with a host of excuses or reasons, finding someone else to do it, or trying to schedule for another time. She finally learned to say, "'I don't want to do it," and, to her, that should be enough.

That *is* enough.

"Self-care is really rooted in self-preservation."

—LIZZO[69]

With all this talk about thriving, we can't forget that first, we need to survive, to make sure we meet all our basic needs. Self-care means simply taking care of ourselves. In 2019, recording artist Lizzo wrote an article about self-care, and she asserted, "We have to start being more honest with what we need, and what we deserve, and start serving that to ourselves. It can be a spa day! But for a lot of people, it's more like, I need a mentor. I need someone to talk to. I need to see someone who looks like me that's successful, that's doing the things that I want to do, to know that it's possible."[70] This last point is so critical for Black folks in America.

Self-care is not self-centered or selfish. It doesn't have to be fancy or expensive. We must practice self-care so we can remain healthy and sustain ourselves. Self-care is central to thriving.

QUESTIONS FOR REFLECTION

1. How do you define "self-care"?
2. What practices, habits, or rituals are core to your personal care?

---

69   Lizzo, "Self-Care Has to Be Rooted in Self-Preservation, Not Just Mimosas and Spa Days," *NBC Universal*, April 19, 2019.

70   Ibid.

3. How do you schedule and honor your commitments to yourself as much as the ones you make with other people?
4. How do you create boundaries around your time and energy?
5. How does your relationship to work contribute to or detract from your personal well-being?

CHAPTER 9

REST

———

"In America, I was free only in battle, never free to rest—and he who finds no way to rest cannot long survive the battle."

—JAMES BALDWIN

Having survived and even thrived in the tumult of 2020, I slid into 2021 like a baseball player running for her life toward home plate. "Safe!"

Then I got COVID-19.

I was about to face, for the umpteenth time, the battle between staying "productive" in pursuit of my goals and giving my body the critical rest it needed.

I received my diagnosis a week and a half after I got sick and was already on the mend. Completely losing my sense of taste and smell prompted me to get tested. I received the email about my results at 11 p.m. on January 20, 2021—US presidential inauguration day. I was convinced that an email meant I was negative because that is how I had received my results in the past. Surely if I was positive, someone would be calling. Right?

I opened the email and scanned past a lot of information to get to my result. The word "POSITIVE" shouted at me from the screen. For a few minutes, my brain stopped working; it was just too much to comprehend. Suddenly, the abstract, existential threat that had previously existed "out there" had landed like a flaming bag of poop in the middle of my bedroom.

My first instinct was to call someone, but it was late. I also didn't want to experience what sometimes happens when I reach out at a time like that, which is the "piling on" effect. That happens when the person on the other end of the line projects all their fears and worries on you. You end the call feeling worse than you did in the beginning. So instead of calling, I did the most unproductive thing you can do at 11 p.m. I started Googling. Suddenly all the information about the potential long-term effects of COVID-19 read differently. Permanent loss of taste and smell. Lingering fatigue. Heart problems. Decreased cognitive function. It only took a few minutes for me to get really worked up.

After about thirty minutes, I paused and started talking to myself as I often do.

Charisse, you need to stop. You don't need all this information right now. What you need is to calm down so you can sleep. Focus on what you can control in this moment. Rest is the most accessible thing right now to help you heal, so rest.

I put lavender oil on my pillow, as I do every night, and then put on my sleep mask. I started my recording of a yoga nidra meditation, and within minutes, I drifted into a peaceful sleep.

Deep, sound sleep is often elusive for me. My mind is just very busy, which is one reason I am so attracted to yoga, meditation, yoga nidra, and other mindfulness practices.

I am not alone in my sleeplessness. Most folks are chronically sleep-deprived. This leads to negative effects ranging from depression and weakened immunity to increased risk of high blood pressure, heart disease, stroke, diabetes, and obesity.[71] Black folks are already at increased risk for these diseases, so being sleep-deprived only exacerbates them. At its extreme, sleep deprivation can lead to more accidents of all kinds, including fatal car crashes. Basically, not getting enough high-quality sleep is killing us.

I can't recall exactly when I was first introduced to the practice of yoga nidra, but I have been led in the practice by various yoga teachers over the years. There is no easy way to explain it, and I am by no means an expert, but it is like a guided meditation that leads the practitioner to a state somewhere between awake and asleep.

In September 2020, I had the privilege of delving deeper into the practice during a forty-day experience with yoga nidra and meditation teacher Tracee Stanley. The class was called "Yoga Nidra and the Power of Manifestation." I practiced every night except a night or two during those forty days, and I have continued off and on since then.

One practice that can accompany yoga nidra is creating a *sankalpa*. In her book, *Radiant Rest*, Tracee Stanley describes a *sankalpa* as "a resolve, intention, or affirmation."[72] By responding to a series of questions during my practice

---

71 "More Sleep Would Make Most Americans Happier, Healthier and Safer," American Psychological Association, accessed February 6, 2021.

72 Tracee Stanley, *Radiant Rest: Yoga Nidra for Deep Relaxation and Awakened Clarity* (Boulder: Shambhala, 2021), 46

with Tracee, and refining it over several days, I created the following *sankalpa*: "I trust myself. I make the right commitments, and I honor them. I say 'no' to that which does not serve me and attract abundance." That was the affirmation I needed to improve my ability to discern which opportunities were right for me as a new business owner. The night I received my positive COVID-19 test result, I returned to a simple affirmation that I had used in the past when I was sick: "I am healthy, well, balanced, and whole."

To begin yoga nidra, you lie down, make yourself warm, cozy, and supported, and get really comfortable. You then either guide yourself or are guided by a teacher to focus on your breathing so you can relax. You then take a sensory journey through the body, bringing your awareness, part by part, to each finger, toe, arms, legs, front and back body. The entire process takes about thirty minutes.

Yoga nidra is deeply restorative to me. By focusing on the sensations in my body, I calm my racing thoughts and remember that I am okay. In *Radiant Rest*, Tracee explains, "Deep relaxation practices help us to relax systematically and to bring awareness to all the parts of ourselves that require loving attention."[73] That was why I turned to the practice the night I found out I had COVID-19. I needed to bring awareness to my body and physical health while softening my fear and anxiety about a future that is always unknown.

I had felt cold symptoms two weeks before I found out I had COVID-19 and was already feeling better, working, and getting back into my exercise routine. Learning about the potential long-term effects of the virus gave me pause. I decided to rest more than it felt like I "needed" to because my body needed healing in ways I could not see or feel. It took

---

73   Ibid, 51

me a few days to come to terms with this. After all, I had a one-year-old business to run and a book to complete.

My predicament reminded me of one of the most resonant passages in Octavia Raheem's book, *Gather*:

"Do you ever feel guilty when you rest? When you pause? Where does that guilt come from? For me, the guilt is textured, layered and sometimes chain-like. It's from deep conditioning at an honest, ancestral level. How much can you take? And with how little sustenance can you work? My ancestors lived inside the systemic shackles of these questions and often died under their oppressive weight."[74]

Damn!

Why is it so hard to take a break? As soon as I asked the question, I knew the answer came from all these ideas embedded in our culture:

Sleep when you're dead.

Burn the midnight oil.

Get rich or die trying.

Rise and grind.

Then layer on top of that the mantras drilled into Black folks:

You have to be twice as good.

You have to work twice as hard.

The list of expressions that glorify working ourselves to the bone goes on and on. We live in a culture that ties self-worth to productivity and rewards busyness. This approach to living undermines our ability to devote time and attention to our well-being.

---

74 Octavia Raheem, *Gather* (Octavia F. Raheem, 2020), 85

Keeping all of this in mind, I cleared my calendar of everything but current client engagements and working on my book. The list of things I was putting on hold so I could rest was long, but I knew I was making the right choice. An amazing thing happened. I felt more at ease in my work. It became easier to prioritize. I reached out and chatted with friends more because I needed the connection to not feel alone on top of needing to be physically isolated. Even with COVID-19, my overall sense of well-being improved.

NO ONE IS GOING TO GIVE YOU REST

Performance artist, activist, theologian, and community healer Tricia Hersey is on a mission to change the way we think about rest. More than 335,000 folks are following her organization The Nap Ministry's Instagram page. I think it's safe to say that people are listening to her message.

It all started when Tricia was in divinity school juggling her studies, parenting a six year old, and working to pay the bills. While she was in school, the Black Lives Matter movement was taking root on the heels of the 2013 murder of Eric Garner in New York City. Police officers had placed Garner in an illegal chokehold while he repeatedly said, "I can't breathe" until he lost consciousness.[75] That was when I first remember Black death becoming a hashtag.

All of this, combined with the demands of being a student, made Tricia exhausted. Her remedy was simple—nap, which she did all over campus whenever she could. She eventually had staked out about ten different spots on campus to catch some Z's. She had no idea at the time that she was planting the seeds for a movement.

---

75 "Eric Garner Dies in NYPD Chokehold," A&E Television Networks, accessed February 6, 2021.

As her studies unfolded, she began to see the intersection between her interest in Black liberation theology, womanism, somatics, and community organizing.[76] Being a performance artist who used theater to spread ideas, it only seemed natural to explore the idea of rest as an interactive performance piece. She did an event during which she rested and invited others to nap and rest with her. She thought it was a one-shot deal, but the response was overwhelming. Everyone wanted to know when she would do it again.

That led to Tricia founding The Nap Ministry in 2016. According to its website, The Nap Ministry "examines the liberating power of naps. We engage with the power of performance art, site-specific installations, and community organizing to install sacred and safe spaces for the community to rest together."[77] The Nap Ministry hosts workshops that offer rest as a tool for community healing. The organization believes "rest is a form of resistance and names sleep deprivation as a racial and social justice issue."[78] The Nap Ministry has now curated events for groups of up to one hundred people around the country.

In 2005, researchers at the University of California, San Diego, began a five-year sleep experiment. They were studying slow-wave sleep, which is the restorative period of sleep so key to good health. People are believed to spend 20 percent of their sleep in this period, which they found to be true among white study participants. Black participants, however, only spent 15 percent of the night in this phase of sleep.[79] It is very difficult, scientifically, to isolate

76 "Our Work Has a Framework," The Nap Ministry, accessed February 6, 2021.

77 Ibid.

78 Ibid.

79 Brian Resnick, "The Racial Inequality of Sleep," Atlantic, October 27, 2015.

all the factors that might be contributing to this difference, but I have a theory: Racism and its day-to-day implications for Black people cause toxic stress. If we are more stressed than our white counterparts, having a harder time sleeping seems like an obvious result.

When people ask Tricia Hersey how they can create more time for rest, she empathizes with them. Capitalism depends upon our belief that we need to work ourselves to the bone. Tricia wants us all to know that we have been "bamboozled" and challenges us to reclaim our time. In a conversation with Tracee Stanley on her podcast *Radiant Rest,* she shared an anecdote about her grandmother, who had nine children and migrated to Chicago from Mississippi to escape the terror of the Jim Crow South. Even though she had two jobs, according to Tricia, "she sat on that couch for thirty minutes every day and rested her eyes."[80]

"No one is going to give you rest," she says.[81] We have to take it. We have to value it, schedule it, create boundaries around it, and just take it.

That is exactly what Dr. Reba Peoples decided that she needed to do.

PEACE OUT

"Every Black person in America needs an 'eff you' fund and a side hustle." This philosophy allowed Dr. Reba Peoples to walk away from her job without a plan.

At the time, she was working for a large hospital's psychiatry practice, which felt more like one big revenue-generating

---

80 Tricia Hersey, "Rest–A Meticulous Love Practice with Tricia Hersey of The Nap Ministry," in *Radiant Rest Podcast with Tracee Stanley,* produced by Baron Rinzler, podcast, 16:51.

81 Ibid, 24:03.

machine than patient care. At the hospital, payment was tied to Relative Value Units (RVU). To generate the required number of RVUs, doctors had to pack patients into the day, twenty minutes per patient. If a patient was late, which was common, by the time their vitals were checked, that could leave as few as ten minutes to be with them—to assess and provide guidance and medication, if necessary. Reba explained, "It was just very stressful and disheartening…It wasn't what I went to school to do."

In training, Reba had the time to really understand each person's biopsychosocial formulation, which is a technical term for getting to know them holistically. That includes what's going on physiologically and anything happening in their lives that might be contributing to their anxiety or depression.

One day, Reba started having terrible migraine headaches. She saw a neurologist who could find nothing wrong. She also had her eyes checked. She started taking migraine medication and just kept trying to power through her job. One day, she just passed out in the middle of the clinic. She explained, "The clinic was attached to a hospital, so the medical assistant just wheeled me down to the emergency room from my office. The entire time I'm just wondering, *Oh my gosh, how am I going to reschedule these patients?*" She already had a month-long waiting list for new patients, so getting sick would cause her to fall even farther behind. Rather than think about her health, all she could think about was her workload. That was her first wake-up call.

The second was a conversation she had with the supervising physician at a new job she got with an outpatient practice. One day, he berated Reba, yelling at her like she was a child. "That was the absolute last straw for me," she said. She turned in her resignation the next day without knowing what she would do next.

When I asked her what she did to heal and recover from that entire experience, she said simply, "Rest." She took a year to rest and plot her next steps. "I think Western culture has this belief that we are not worthy, or we're not valuable if we're not producing something. So just taking that time to rest and read and just simply be was probably the most invaluable thing for me," she explained. Her "eff you" fund gave her the freedom to do that.

During that time, she began to envision her private practice, Imara Health and Wellness. As her practice evolves, she is working primarily with visionary Black women who want to make a larger impact on the world, but things like fear, self-doubt, depression, or anxiety are holding them back from reaching their full potential. She has created a framework called S.M.A.R.T. Wellness that helps patients focus on the things they can control, like getting enough sleep and exercise.

In describing the framework, Reba explains, "It not only helps high-achieving Black women focus on the basics of self-care, but it also helps them learn to reprogram old patterns that no longer serve their growth or emotional wellbeing." She also notes that healing happens in the community, and her unique approach "invites cultural wisdom, spirituality, and civic action into the collective experience of healing racialized trauma." She is finding great meaning in this approach and finds it to be transformative for the women she works with.

In terms of nutrition, she doesn't just focus on diet and supplements, though those things are important. For her, nourishment is also "what you're feeding your body and what you're feeding your consciousness. Any kind of media I consume has to be something that's going to really be in service of growth, rather than something that fuels fear or insecurity or inadequacy."

Talking to Reba was so good for me. Whenever I feel worn out, anxious, or burnt out, I say to myself, *Charisse, just get back to basics.* The basics are all the things Reba includes in her S.M.A.R.T. Wellness guide.

I interviewed Reba in the fall of 2020, and when I asked if she felt like she was personally thriving, she said, "I do. I mean, in spite of everything that's happening, I have a strange sense of contentment." Her response made me think of what I felt for much of 2020. A lot was going on in the world. There was ongoing racist violence and oppression and an additional layer of suffering and death caused by the pandemic. I had to remind myself that it was okay to be okay. It is not a betrayal of anyone who is suffering more to thrive while Black.

SABBATICAL

The first time I really took a sabbatical, I didn't call it that. It was just time off between my job and starting my first business, a nonprofit consulting practice. It was a six-week break, and I spent a month in Puerto Rico studying Spanish. Class was only three hours a day, so there was plenty of time to hang out and explore. It was both restful and rejuvenating.

The word "sabbatical" can be traced back to the word "sabbath," which literally means "rest."[82] In reality it's rarely practiced. If we're not working at our jobs, we're cooking, cleaning, running errands, and the list goes on and on. There is just so much to *do*, right? It escapes most of us, especially in

---

82   "Sabbath," Merriam-Webster, Incorporated, accessed February 6, 2021.

the West, that we're doing much of what we do poorly and not enjoying it because we're so worn out. And when it comes to work, forget it. The only workers who routinely receive paid sabbaticals are professors, and it's not really rest. It's time off from teaching so they can do more research or writing so they can land on the right side of the equation, "publish or perish." For hourly employees, vacations aren't even possible, let alone a sabbatical. Only 31 percent of the lowest earners even have paid sick leave.[83]

In 2019, I took a real, three-month, unpaid sabbatical. It wasn't easy to give myself permission to do it at first because I had no income and was about to start a new business, but I knew it would be good for me. During that time, I did not allow myself to work much other than doing my coaching certification program.

In case you're wondering—no, I do not have a trust fund. I did something radical. I quit my job, sold my house, and used some earnings to fund my time off and invest in my new venture. When I returned to the country, that's when I moved in with my cousin Kanika and family for a year and a half.

During my sabbatical, I went on a highly anticipated adventure. I boarded a plane to Amsterdam with a return ticket from Marrakech five weeks later and nothing planned in between. I snaked my way through Europe by train and flew down to Morocco, figuring everything out as I went. It was one of the most exhilarating and terrifying things I have done in my life! I encountered amazing people and ate interesting food, all while practicing my Spanish and French. I saw breathtaking sights and took gorgeous photos.

---

83 Drew DeSilver, "As Coronavirus Spreads, Which U.S. Workers Have Paid Sick Leave–and Which Don't?" *Pew Research Center*, March 12, 2020.

I successfully navigated getting lost and numerous other frustrating situations by being aware, asking for help, and trusting my instincts.

During this sabbatical, I also traveled to Germany to meet my brother Christian, niece Ricarda, and nephew Lennard for the very first time ever! Explaining this would require an entire book, but, needless to say it was incredible and surreal.

I love travel because it gives me a fresh perspective on my life and work. I would rather spend money on travel than anything else. I have intentionally kept my living expenses relatively low so I can spend any surplus on experiences like this.

Yes, this was a privilege. I had an asset to sell and money to afford health care and meet my basic needs. I planned and I sacrificed. I understand many folks don't have the option of taking a sabbatical. But I know so many people who do but are afraid. More than half of American workers don't even use all their paid vacation days every year.[84] So much stigma is attached to leaving the workforce for even a short while. If you are climbing the corporate ladder, if you leave your rung, you could come back and find that you have been replaced. Even women who go on maternity leave are punished. The entire world of work is broken.

We all have different values, obligations, and life circumstances that drive our decisions about work. I have some big career dreams that I will work hard to achieve. But those aren't the only dreams that matter to me. I want to be healthy and well and have a life filled with joy. So, despite the risks and the sacrifices, the sabbatical was 100 percent worth it. It gave me everything I needed to start my new business with renewed

---

84 Meghan McCarty Carino, "American Workers Can Suffer Vacation Guilt … If They Take Vacations at All," *Marketplace*, July 12, 2019.

energy and focus. The adventure was expensive, but the rewards were priceless. I am incredibly grateful for the privilege.

I was reminded of a story that multidisciplinary artist Fahamu Pecou told me about some time he spent in South Africa for a printmaking residency. The director, master printmaker Malcolm Christian, gathered everyone around and explained his philosophy for helping artists find more creative space. He started talking to the group about the word "inspiration," which comes from the Latin *inspirare*, "to breathe" or "blow into."[85] Christian announced that in order to access inspiration, they would have to spend the next twenty-four hours in complete silence. They were also told not to create anything. Malcolm described the practice of creativity as analogous to breathing. Production is the exhale, while the silence he was imposing was like the inhale. Fahamu reflected, "We are often so focused on the output we neglect to reinvest in ourselves with stillness and silence. The moments of pause are necessary to maintain a healthy balance in all things."

What a beautiful analogy.

"If you are not resting, you will not make it. I need you to make it."

—THE NAP MINISTRY[86]

Rest takes many forms outside of sleeping and napping. I try to spend some time every day just staring into space, sometimes listening to music, but making sure I am not looking at my phone or my laptop. Doing social media fasts

---

85 "Inspiration," Merriam-Webster, Incorporated, accessed March 11, 2021.

86 The Nap Ministry (@thenapministry), "A Care and Justice Strategy," Instagram photo, September 30, 2020.

can also help us rest from overstimulation and unhealthy comparisons. Getting outside during the day for fresh air and connecting with nature can be a great way to get rest and rejuvenate.

My favorite and most accessible form of rest is meditation. All it takes is a few moments of still, quiet, and long, deep breaths.

Anything that gets us off autopilot and allows us time to reconnect with ourselves can be restful. It doesn't matter what form of rest you take; all that matters is that you take it.

QUESTIONS FOR REFLECTION

1. How does your body tell you that it needs rest?
2. What activities, in addition to sleep, do you find restful? How often do you engage in them?
3. What physical locations make you feel peaceful and at ease? How often do you go there?
4. What simple things can you do in your home to make the space feel more relaxing and conducive to rest?
5. If you have paid vacation days that you don't have plans to use, reflect on the reasons why. How can you shift your thinking and give yourself permission to take time off?

CHAPTER 10

JOY

———

"As Black people, our lives are not tragedies. I will keep fighting against that narrative. Our lives are survival stories that have been passed down from generation to generation. These stories are about joy and celebration and our inherent power. No one has the capacity to steal our joy."

—DIRIYE OSMAN

When I met Delroy in January 2020, he was going through a rough time. His business was experiencing growing pains, and he was grappling with how to find more fulfillment outside of his work as an industrial engineer. We met at TGS, where we were working side by side in the restaurant. We struck up a conversation and immediately hit it off, talking about life, leadership, and the challenges of entrepreneurship.

We talked a few times and fell out of touch for several months. When we eventually checked in, Delroy was in the midst of some radical life changes. The coronavirus pandemic,

he said, was "the last nail in the coffin." He had recently finished a series of client engagements and realized that he no
longer had any distinction between work and the rest of his
life. Often working until 1:30 a.m. trying to get caught up, his
energy was flagging, and he could not muster the motivation
he once had for his business. Delroy was just going through
the motions and knew it was time to make a change.

Owning land was always on Delroy's bucket list. He said,
"That is the epitome of a life well-lived. Having your own land
and being able to pass it down. That is something unfortu-
nately no one in my family has been able to do."

Having grown up in Jamaica, Delroy was accustomed to
having fruit trees around. Eating things growing right outside of
his home was normal. That was not the case when he moved to
the US. He didn't start growing things on his own until he was
in his late twenties. At the time, he was living in an apartment
in Boston that had a small balcony. He planted a little tomato
plant that turned into twenty, completely taking over the space.
Every morning, he walked out onto the eight-by-four-foot space
before he started his day. He thought to himself, even though
it is a small space, "I'm gonna make it my little slice of heaven."

He eventually moved to Atlanta, where he had a little
garden growing green peppers, jalapeños, hot peppers, and
pumpkins. He loved going outside and walking into his garden to see what was growing. He couldn't wait to grow more.
He told me, "I think as Black people, especially, we've tried
to run so far away from any kind of agrarian culture. Having
my hand in the dirt literally planting a seed and watching
it grow, to create an environment where plants can flourish,
there's no better definition of a home."

I hadn't given much thought to Black people's modern
relationship to farming, but it makes so much sense. Black

folks were brought to the Americas to work on farms under brutal conditions with no pay. After slavery, no one got forty acres and a mule. Many families remained indentured servants, incurring debts that were literally impossible to pay off. The land became a prison more than a symbol of freedom.

Ever since I moved to Atlanta in 2007, I have become increasingly fascinated by Black farmers. I once heard one say that growing your own food is like printing your own money. I have loved that expression ever since.

Halfway through 2020, Delroy started exploring real estate investments to create additional streams of revenue. He wasn't looking for a home for himself. A friend of his sent him an email about a house with about seven acres of land. He explained, "I saw the house; I saw the land. Within fifteen seconds, I heard a voice in my head that said, *This is it.*" He called his realtor and went to view the property the next day.

Four months after seeing the property for the first time, Delroy moved into his new homestead. Months later, it all still felt too good to be true. He shared, "I just cannot believe that I was able to do this thing that I've been wanting to do for so long. It felt like it was so far off."

Delroy's vision is much bigger than him. His goal is to have a sustainable farm that grows enough food for fifty families. He also wants to construct indoor-outdoor spaces where people can learn about farming and sustainable living. He told me:

"I'm destined for something important. I don't know what that is yet, but I want to be ready for it, and I don't want to feel like I have to sacrifice my health, my joy, my body, my everything."

The farm is helping him find his way back from stressed and overworked to a more peaceful, joyful life.

Delroy is slowly planning, renovating, and getting used to raising animals, including five Nubian goats, a donkey, and some chickens. He also added a chocolate labrador retriever, named Koffee after his favorite reggae singer, to the family. Every morning he wakes up at 6 a.m. and feeds the animals. Then he spends about twenty minutes walking the property. He explained, "I try to walk somewhere else new every other morning. I just literally like to take it all in, every cranny, every tree. I try to find something new about the property that I didn't know before."

The last time we talked, he was in such a good place, and he lit up talking about his new home and the lifestyle that accompanies it. "I've been in a space of just thankfulness. I've been so thankful every morning I get up. On mornings like this, where it was sunny and beautiful and just looking at the trees cast their shadows— all I'm saying is 'thank you, thank you, thank you.'"

MISS COOL

The bass was bumpin', and my hips were windin.' David Hinds, from the band Steel Pulse, was crooning one of my favorite songs. My head dropped and my eyes closed as I fell deeper and deeper into the music. I lifted my arms and swayed as time and space fell away. A voice saying, "Ma'am? Ma'am?! May I take your order?" snapped me back to reality.

It was time to order my coffee.

I love dancing. I always have. Any time. Any place. Whenever I hear music playing, I have to move. It's like I literally can't help it. Dancing brings me so much joy. My uncle Mitch was so tickled by my dancing when I was a little girl that he nicknamed me "Miss Cool." I would do the same thing I did at the coffee shop, head down, braids dangling, lost in the music and my own world.

I had formal dance training off and on growing up, starting when I was in pre-school, attending Mayfair Academy on the South Side of Chicago. In elementary school at St. Thomas Apostle, I took "African dance" with Mr. Marshall Lindsey. I put "African" in quotes because Africa is a huge content with thousands of dance styles. And as far as I can remember, we performed the same dance every year, Fanga, a West African dance popularized in the US by the pioneering dancer Pearl Primus.[87] I continued to study West African dance in Chicago with Abdoulaye Camara, also known as "Papa."

When I wasn't in a dance class, I was at a party dancing to House music. It is impossible to describe the late eighties, early nineties house scene in Chicago. All I can say is that everyone danced, and the dance floor was like the United Nations: men, women, gay, and straight people dressed in a diverse array of styles, sometimes in costumes, but donning nothing that would interfere with the number one mission: dancing. Together we formed an undulating sea, overflowing with freedom and joy.

I continued dancing when I got to college, and through dance, I met Jasán Ward.

DANCING BETWEEN HEARTACHE AND JOY

Jasán has been through a lot. Reflecting on his life, he shared, "I think I am here to create some kind of change for people living with HIV and for little Black gay boys who

---

87 "Dance of the African Diaspora Pearl Primus," Jacob's Pillow Dance Festival, accessed March 11, 2021.

may have been afraid of their sexuality, maybe they're not so afraid anymore."

"For me, to thrive means to wake up every day and rise above anything that may keep me from wanting to get out of bed, put my feet on the ground, stand up and go to the bathroom and wash my face." That was Jasán's response to the first question I asked everyone I interviewed. Learning what he had to go through every day to keep putting one foot in front of the other humbled me.

Jasán and I went to Cornell University together and danced in Uhuru Kuumba Dance Ensemble. We didn't know each other extremely well, but I remembered Jasán's bright light, energy, hard work, and beautiful dancing. After Cornell, we lost touch for many years. I vaguely remembered stories about how his tenure at Cornell ended, but I paid them no mind.

Decades later, Jasán and I reconnected on Facebook. I continued to follow him from a distance as he shared about his life and work and watched videos that he posted of himself dancing in his living room. Through Facebook, I learned he had been living with HIV since 1995. He was dedicating his life to spreading awareness about the disease, even becoming a spokesmodel for HIV Stops With Me. All I could think was, *What a brave, brilliant, beautiful soul.*

In June 2019, Jasán created a private Facebook group and invited me to join. He wrote the following in the group description: "For so many years, I lived in fear and was ashamed of being HIV positive. I will not live in fear or be ashamed of being a person who now has cancer. I am scared. I am hopeful. I am angry. I am a fighter. I will need an army to get through this journey. Please do not respond with 'I'm so sorry' comments. Instead, post something funny, a link to a cool website, lists of books you recommend, music that is moving your soul and shuffling your feet, protein shake recipes, Netflix recommendations."[88]

I was deeply honored to be in the group and, like all the others, sprang into action, offering what I could. Following that, Jasán was on my mind a lot more. I watched with reverence as he vulnerably shared his journey through chemo, the good days, the bad days, the highs and the lows. Over time, he got stronger and stronger until his treatment was done, and he was cancer-free.

When I reached out to Jasán to interview him, it was amazing to speak to him after all those years. What I learned blew me away. When he was diagnosed with HIV, he was told that he had four months to live. After that, he said he felt like he was just "gliding through life." Something shifted for him when he turned forty in 2012. He said he just looked up and thought, "Oh my gosh, I'm still here!" Everything changed for him after that. He thought to himself, "I'm never looking back. I am only looking forward."

Jasán spent much of his adult life working to improve the lives of people living with HIV and help prevent its spread. He has been a case manager and test counselor doing work around HIV prevention and awareness in lesbian, gay, bisexual, and transgender communities of color. He worked at the New York State Task Force on Black Gay Men's Health, and in that role, he was invited to the White House three times during the Obama Administration.

At one point in his career, Jasán worked in communications and fundraising for Garth Fagan Dance. They used one

---

88 Jasán Ward, "LIFE: Love. Intention. Focus. Empowerment," Facebook, June 28, 2019.

night of their fall performance to raise money for Broadway Cares, which funds HIV/AIDS organizations. Three hours before the performance, the executive director asked him if he would be willing to give a speech that evening. As Jasán told me the story, his face lit up and I could see the joy the memory invoked. In his speech, he shared his story and how lucky he had been to have access to great health care, but many people aren't that lucky, which is why he implored them to donate.

One would never know how shy Jasán is, given the very public roles he's been in. When he does public speaking, he said he's "drenched from head to toe." When people ask him why he does it, he says, "Because I have to. You know it'll pass, but the impact that I can have by standing in front of a room and saying something for ten minutes can help change someone's life." He went on to say, "I knew that I was meant to be in that room."

Even when Jasán is talking about sad and painful things, he exudes palpable joy and light. He told me, "I'm really balancing being happy and miserable at the same time; I think you can have both and still continue to thrive." When life knocks Jasán down, he gets back up repeatedly with grace, joy, vulnerability, and humility.

"There is something in me that is, I guess, at its core really positive and good and hopeful. That's what I always try to tap into because I live with darkness too. And sometimes the darkness has won, you know, but I've been able to get that light back and make it stronger than the darkness."

Jasán never got to earn his degree from Cornell, but eventually went back to school. He learned that he had cancer two days before he could finally walk across the stage to receive his undergraduate degree. The news was devastating. He was in immense pain, but he didn't tell anyone right away. He just wanted to make it through the graduation. As he was getting ready to line up, a young man approached him and said, "Hey, I know you." It turns out that Jasán had been his caseworker at an organization providing services to homeless and displaced people. The man told him, "I went to the dentist because of you. I was able to find a job because of you. And now I'm graduating and going to get my master's once I'm done with this." It was one of many times in Jasán's life that he was reminded why he was here and why it was worth it to stay hopeful and keep fighting. His strength had inspired others.

At the end of our conversation in 2020, I learned that Jasán's cancer had returned. He was facing some major decisions about if he would go through treatment again and, if so, which treatment he would take. I could not process the fact that he was saying "if" he went through treatment again. I knew that Jasán didn't want my pity or sympathy. He told me, "I'm still finding joy and happiness, you know, and I still want to thrive, and I still want to do things. I'm not feeling defeated."

#BLACKJOYMATTERS

I learned a lot about joy from Delroy and Jasán. Life is full of hard work, stressors, and pain. Sometimes it's easy to find joy in the little things, but sometimes you have to really work for it. I don't believe that "joy" is the same as "happiness." Emotions are fleeting. Joy is a perspective, a worldview, a choice. The more you seek, the more you find.

Celebrating Black joy is a movement. Seeing the simple phrase "Black joy" lit the spark that led me to write an entire book in a year when Black folks were experiencing a lot of collective pain. In the process of following the "Black joy" hashtag down the proverbial rabbit hole, I even stumbled upon the Black Joy Parade in Oakland, California. It describes itself as being "hyper-positive" in its celebration of the Black experience and contributions to history and culture.[89] Hopefully, I'll go someday.

My research also led me to the Black Joy Archive. Founded in May 2020, it had a simple call to action: Submit images of joy. It pronounced, "The goal is that this collective action can be an outlet for Black individuals to heal through lifting our voices and giving space for our experiences to be seen, while also demystifying the notion that black lives can solely be viewed in a negative vacuum of struggle."[90]

The images include Black folks hugging, laughing, celebrating, jumping rope, hanging out at the beach, kissing, and just posing looking fly. They showcase our pride, resilience, and our joy. The joy drips from the photos like honey, and I am here for every last drop.

QUESTIONS FOR REFLECTION

1. How do you define joy?
2. What brings you joy, and how can you make more time for it?
3. How can you find joy in your heart, even when life is really hard?
4. Who do you admire for their joyful spirit?
5. How can you infuse your day with joy as soon as you wake up in the morning?

---

89   "Mission," Black Joy Parade, accessed March 11, 2021.
90   Black Joy Archive, accessed March 11, 2021.

One way Jasán spreads joy is by sharing his poetry with the world. I am grateful to be able to share one of his pieces with you.

49

Here
I am
Bright
Chiclet grin
Hiding
Darkness
Soaking up
Sweetness
Wounded
Tender soul
Quiet
Yet, living
Loud
With
Courage
Intention
Love
Half century
On the near
Horizon
Gliding on
Hope
Rising...above
Fear
-JMW

CHAPTER 11

PUTTING IT INTO PRACTICE

"Everything is practice."

—PELÉ

I don't know a lot about soccer, but if the man widely considered to be the greatest player of all time, Pelé, tells us that "everything is practice," I think we can trust it.

Thriving is practice. You have to experiment. If you try something that doesn't work, you ditch it and move onto something else, building upon what you learned. When you find what works, you do it repeatedly until it becomes second nature. The practice never ends.

This chapter will help you take action to cultivate the conditions to help you thrive more.

START WITH PURPOSE

There is a lot of talk about "finding one's purpose," but I don't think it's something that you have to go hunting for.

As Chadwick Boseman said, "It is the reason you are on the planet at this particular time in history."[91] Some people fear that when they identify their "purpose," they have to run out and look for a new job or start their own business. That may be the case for some, but probably not most people.

Clarifying your purpose could help you find meaning in what you are already doing. It could help you deepen the impact that you want to have on others as you move through your day-to-day life.

EXERCISE:

Try writing a purpose or mission statement. If it's helpful, explore this formula: Who you are + how you want to feel + what you are good at *and* love to do + what the world needs.

Don't get hung up on the difference between "purpose," "mission," and "vision." I have literally spent hours in strategic planning meetings debating the distinctions with former nonprofit clients. Just use the word that resonates with you. You could even call it your "manifesto." As long as you understand your intentions, that's all that matters.

Here is my mission statement: *I am an author, coach, and speaker; my mission is to live a joyful, connected, and prosperous life and to use my talents, strengths, and life experiences to help others do the same.*

Pretty simple, right? But life can be so full of events that distract us from our mission and purpose. Because of that, I added the following to my mission as a reminder:

---

91   Chadwick Boseman, "Chadwick Boseman's Howard University 2018 Commencement Speech," Howard University, May 12, 2018, YouTube video, 31:46.

Everything I do personally and professionally is connected to my mission, including:

- *developing a productive mindset*
- *working out*
- *eating healthy*
- *maintaining good relationships with family and friends*
- *doing yoga and meditating*
- *managing my finances*
- *making time for rest and contemplation*
- *being of service*
- *having fun and playing*
- *being completely present and prepared for every client*
- *writing* The Joy of Thriving While Black
- *teaching my coaching students*
- *creating content*
- *developing and offering experiences, including workshops and retreats*

My intention, day in and day out, is to show up for my mission in the best way I can.

That last sentence is so important. I am not trying to be perfect, only to do the best I can.

Having a simple mission statement can provide a "North Star" to guide short-term goals and major life decisions. I have my statement framed on my altar, and I read it to myself regularly.

I have reminders like this for myself everywhere. I have Post-its on my mirror, notes above my desk, and affirmations taped to my laptop. I even have one of those grooved blackboards with the little plastic letters that you can move around to write messages. As I write this, my board says, "My mind is open, clear, focused, and creative." I created that when I had writer's block. Additionally, every year, I create a vision board, and it is a serious project and work of art.

Why do I do all this? Because it's so easy to forget all the things I want to be, do, and remember! Posting reminders everywhere keep me on track. If you haven't tried it already, give it a try.

A FRAMEWORK FOR GROWTH AND CHANGE

As a leadership coach, I help my clients by asking questions that allow me to support them on their paths to achieving their goals. I learned this framework through JRNI, or "journey," Life Coaching. I teach it to coaching students and use it to coach clients and myself.[92]

You can journal your answers to the questions below to explore the themes in this book. Start with the theme that seems right to you.

You can begin with just free writing, then once you read what you've written, you can add more clarity and detail.

I will walk you through an example below with "Imani," with some commentary to help you dig even deeper. Imagine that the parts in italics are her answers.

WHERE ARE YOU NOW?

The current state of your life relative to your problem, goal, or the change that you are seeking.

Between parenting, my job, being a partner and maintaining a household, life just feels so demanding. I am in a loving relationship and my job is okay, but it just seems like I can never get enough done. I am so stressed that I'm just not

---

92   "Our Mission Is Simple Helping Adventurous Life Coaches Launch Thriving Practices," JRNI, accessed March 12, 2021.

enjoying life the way I want to. It's like I'm a slave to my to-do list and have forgotten how to have fun. I find myself asking, "Is this all there is?" I feel guilty because I think I should just be more grateful for what I have. Something just feels off. I believe life can be better than this.

COMMENTARY

Once you take a stab at responding to the first question, see if you can find places where you can define things even more. What does it feel like to be "stressed"? How does that show up in your body?

WHERE DO YOU WANT TO BE?

This is where you envision your desired future state. What do you want your life to look like? How do you want to feel? How do you want to be spending your time and with whom? Use all your senses. Give yourself space to dream without worrying about how to get there. This can be hard! If you get stuck, think of everything you don't want and then envision the opposite.

I honestly just want to feel happier and more free. I want to enjoy the time that I'm not working more. I want more quality time with my family and more "me" time. I want to laugh more and daydream. I want to wander without always being tied to my schedule. I want to explore the city more and get off the beaten path. I want to feel proud of what I'm contributing and feel good about myself. I also want to feel like sometimes it's enough to just "be." At the end of each day, I want to lay my head down and know that what I have done was enough.

Again, start by finding things to define. What does it look like to "feel more free?" What does "quality time" with family entail, and what might you do with your "me time"?

This short paragraph represents many desires, right? Sometimes envisioning the future can be like opening Pandora's box. If you articulate your vision, it might seem, at first, like it's unattainable. However, this can be the fun, creative part. When you're imagining the future, the sky's the limit! By envisioning what you want in as much detail as possible, you can eventually take steps to get there.

WHAT STEPS CAN YOU TAKE TO MOVE CLOSER TO YOUR GOALS?

This is about action. There are so many right ways to move forward. There is no perfect next step. It's important that you just start. You might take two steps forward and one step back. You might take a wrong turn. It's all a part of the process.

One of the things that makes me feel relaxed, happy, and free is getting out into nature. That accomplishes so much of what I just described. I could plan a day trip with my family, pack a yummy lunch, and just spend a few hours at the state park outside of the city walking and exploring—not watching the clock, not on our cell phones, just enjoying our time.

COMMENTARY

Great action items are specific and time bound like this. The sooner you can define a small action, the sooner you can begin moving toward your vision. My friend Raquiba gave me one of my all-time favorite mantras: "Motivation follows action." Start taking steps and the motivation and inspiration will follow. Remember to take it one day at a time, and it's all practice.

WHAT OBSTACLES CAN YOU FORESEE TO TAKING THOSE STEPS?

This is pretty straightforward. By anticipating roadblocks, you can address them in advance and increase your chances of success.

I've got to talk to my partner about the day trip and get it on the calendar. We might have to look out a few weeks to find a date where we don't have any conflicts. To be honest, the biggest roadblock is in my mind. Even though I think this will be good for me, there is a voice in my head that says this isn't a good use of time. I could be grocery shopping, cleaning, or doing something more productive to prepare for the week.

COMMENTARY

This question helps you break your action into smaller steps. Sometimes we can be hard on ourselves for not following through on our plans when in reality, what we thought was one action is actually ten. We just have to break it down.

HOW CAN YOU OVERCOME THOSE OBSTACLES?

I can remember my vision and why it's important to create this time for myself.

COMMENTARY

The practical hurdles were addressed well here. The voice in Imani's head that said, "This isn't a good use of time" is a limiting belief. I address those in detail below.

WHERE CAN YOU GO FOR SUPPORT?

This can be people in your life like a spouse, partner, family, or friends. It can be organizations, clubs, or a faith organization. Coaches, therapists, and support groups are great. Online resources, books, and articles can also be helpful.

My partner, Isaiah, is my biggest support, and I know he'll be into this. I could also start reading all those hiking e-newsletters I subscribe to but stopped paying attention to. The stories and photos inspire me. I love geeking out over the camping and hiking equipment too!

COMMENTARY

This goes back to my note about posting reminders everywhere. There is a positive psychology concept called "immersion." In his book, *The Talent Code: Greatness Isn't Born. It's Grown. Here's How,* journalist Daniel Coyle writes about his research into maximizing potential. In one chapter, he explores how Brazil produces so many great soccer players. On a short walk down a street in Brazil, he noticed fifty symbols related to the sport, from flags and t-shirts to people playing in the street and people watching the game in a bar.[93] We can replicate this for ourselves by putting symbols of what we most want for ourselves all around us.

HOW WILL YOU HOLD YOURSELF ACCOUNTABLE?

How will you increase your chances of following through? You could tell a friend or get an accountability partner. This is proven to help! Put whatever you've committed to in your calendar and treat the appointment with yourself like you would if it were with someone else.

After working out the timing and logistics, I'll just put the trip to the state park on the calendar. I'm giving myself one week to schedule it.

---

93 Bakari Akil, "The Power of Positive Immersion–Is Your Environment Right for You?" *Psychology Today*, February 4, 2010.

COMMENTARY

Accountability is important, but don't be too rigid about it. That will only produce more stress.

HOW WILL YOU CELEBRATE?

This is so important! You can simply acknowledge your win to yourself and give yourself a pat on the back. You could track wins in your journal or planner every day. I am a huge fan of that. The practice literally changed my life. Or you could throw yourself a party! However you want to celebrate, do it. This is how we keep ourselves inspired and motivated. When we celebrate all that is working and good, we rewire our brain from a negativity bias to one of gratitude. It fuels hope and optimism.

There is a lookout in the woods that we used to go to a long time ago. When you talk, you hear an incredible echo. We love to go there and yell! We can do that as a celebration of how good it feels to be there. We can also take beautiful photos and look at them when we get home to remind us of how precious the time was.

COMMENTARY

I don't know about you, but I am feeling super excited for Imani!

If this sounds like a lot of questions and steps, don't worry. You actually go through parts of this process all the time in your mind even though it may not always be intentional or conscious. Having your dreams swirling around in your head, but no plans written down, can cause overwhelm and the feeling of being "stuck." If you take these steps, write them down and talk them out with someone; it gets easier and easier.

Any example like this in writing is intrinsically oversimplified. You probably can't answer these questions in one sitting, but that is a good thing. Ongoing self-reflection is a practice in and of itself.

Change is not easy, but engaging your deepest desires to spark you into action can help. This takes commitment, which can be fueled by returning to your vision repeatedly. Immerse yourself in your vision!

OVERCOMING LIMITING BELIEFS

As you continue on your path, growing, stretching, evolving, you will encounter limiting beliefs. Remember Imani's limiting belief? Her major barrier to planning a trip to the state park with her family was the thought that she *should* spend that time doing something more "productive."

Below are some limiting beliefs and ways to reframe theme. These reframes are some of many options. Think of your own examples as you're reading.

Limiting Belief: This will never work. I've tried over and over again, and I keep failing.

Reframe: Every time I have failed, I have learned something that could help me succeed the next time. I am proud of myself and my persistence. There are still things I haven't tried. I believe that change is possible, so I'll keep going.

Limiting Belief: Black people aren't successful at _____, or don't do _____.

Reframe: Is that a fact or a feeling? If anyone has done it before, it is possible that I can. I have few role models, but I can seek them out and build a network of supports and mentors who can help me along my way. Being literally the first Black person is something to be proud of. Think of Vice President Kamala Harris, who represents three "firsts" in her role: woman, Black, and Indian American. Remember her refrain inspired by her mother, "While I may be the first woman in this office, I will not be the last."[94]

Limiting Belief: I don't have time.

Reframe: "I don't have time" really means "this is not a priority." I have twenty-four hours in the day like everyone else. Because this is a priority for me, I will make the time. I will find something else to sacrifice, like binge-watching Netflix or mindlessly scrolling on social media. My vision is worth the trade-off.

Limiting Belief: I don't deserve this.

Note: This limiting belief is sneaky! We rarely say this to ourselves explicitly, but deep down inside, we might feel unworthy of joy, happiness, and thriving. After all, when so many are suffering, how dare you be happy? Survivor's guilt is so common, especially among middle-class Black folks who come from humble beginnings.

Reframe: I deserve to be happy and to thrive just because I exist. That is not a *betrayal* of the Black experience but a *celebration* of it. I want this for myself and can be a role model for others. It is my responsibility to thrive. The fact that I even have access to *The Joy of Thriving While Black* and am making the time to contemplate these questions is a miracle. I am my ancestor's wildest dreams!

---

94 Lauren Gambino, "'I won't be the last': Kamala Harris, first woman elected US vice-president, accepts place in history," *The Guardian*, November 8, 2020.

ON SELF-COMPASSION AND PATIENCE

If you want thrive more, you have to change something. Change can be hard. Learning and growth are uncomfortable. One of the best things you can do is be gentle and compassionate with yourself. Talk to yourself like you would talk to a friend.

One of my favorite self-love practices is writing love letters to myself. I don't usually plan it. I just do it when I need a boost or want to override some negative self-talk.

Because 2020 was challenging in so many ways, I started including a little love note at the top of my quarterly goals to remind me to extend myself extra grace:

Dear Charisse,

You created these goals in a period of high motivation, inspiration, and clarity in the midst of a global pandemic. You are going to do your absolute best, recognizing there will be ups and downs. You will continue to ride the waves. Some of these things may carry over into the next quarter, and that's okay.

I am proud of you, and I believe in you. You have come so far in your ability to envision what you want and chart a path to get there. Among other things, this year you have started a business and written a book. Girl! You are so amazing.

As you look forward to the next quarter, remember to be gentle with yourself. You are learning to live alone again at a time when your movement in the world is seriously restricted. First and foremost, take really good care of yourself! Use all your resources and prioritize connecting with other people. When you feel lost, get still, be quiet, and ask for guidance. Beneath the surface, there is always an answer. The entire universe is conspiring to help you!

Just remember, no matter what, I love you so much, and I am always here for you.

Love,
Me

The idea of writing a love letter to yourself might make you cringe, and that's okay. Have you ever written a love letter to someone else? If so, why not do something similar for yourself?

WE'RE IN THIS TOGETHER

I once heard that you should teach what you most want to learn. I think that's why I became a yoga teacher, a coach, and a teacher of coaches. That's part of what drove me to write this book. I am still learning.

Overall, I am thriving, but it is not a static state. Every day I work on my mindset, habits, actions, and building community. Some days are better than others.

I really hope these stories inspire you. I also hope you learn some new things about thriving and reflect on how they relate to your life. I hope the questions and exercises in this chapter give you some practical tools you can use on your journey. Finally, I hope that you believe, with all your heart, that you can thrive.

You are strong and resilient, and you can let others support you. Be proud of who you are! Build community and help others along the way. Keep exploring and living your purpose. Rest and take good care of yourself.

Last, but not least, remember that everything is practice.

AUTHOR'S NOTE

—

"The new dawn blooms as we free it, for there is always light if only we're brave enough to see it, if only we're brave enough to be it."

—AMANDA GORMAN

When I began writing *The Joy of Thriving While Black* in the summer of 2020, the Atlanta days were bright and hot, but also somehow dark.

I am one of the lucky ones. By pulling together with family and friends, I navigated the fear and uncertainty and even survived catching the coronavirus.

Though I attempted to explain it in my introduction, the truth is, there is no rational explanation for why I wrote a book in the middle of my first year in business during a global pandemic. Then again, art and creativity are not rational pursuits.

I began this project with a lot of joy, hope, and excitement, but the deeper I got into it, the more I questioned my sanity. My interviews were the highlights of this experience. However, the months of writing and revising were often long and lonely.

Near the end, I battled doubt and fear, wondering if I had wasted ten months of my life on a flight of fancy.

Yet, here I sit, just a few days shy of the first day of spring. It is a beautiful seventy-three degrees, and the birds are chatty. The foliage on the hill facing the Atlanta Beltline outside of my apartment is turning green. I am different in ways that will probably take me a long time to understand.

In less than two months, I will hold a copy of *The Joy of Thriving While Black* in my hands. I have no idea what will happen after that. All I know is that right now, in this moment, I am grateful for the journey and everyone who has walked with me.

Charisse M. Williams
Atlanta, Georgia
March 11, 2021

ACKNOWLEDGMENTS

I had no idea how many people were involved in writing and publishing a book until I embarked on this journey. I am overwhelmed with gratitude.

Thank you to everyone who granted me an interview. There would be no book without your time, energy, and generosity with your stories.

I also could not have done this without my amazing clients. By trusting me as your coach, you helped me believe I had something to say that others would want to hear.

I offer my deepest, heartfelt thanks to my father, James Williams, and "Bonus" mom Kathryn Williams for always being my biggest cheerleaders.

I am grateful to my entire family for your love and deep belief in me. Whether we were near or far, I always felt it.

Thank you, Sarah Stanford, for spending the summer of 2020 helping me do research. I appreciate you so much, and I am really proud of you!

To my friends, many of whom I name in this book, thank you for letting me laugh and cry with you over the years.

I also want to thank Eric Koester for your bold vision and beautiful execution of the Creator Institute. There is no way I would have written a book without your structure and guidance. I am especially grateful for my developmental editor Jem Chambers-Black who gracefully guided me, week by week, through the writing process from the book's inception to the first draft.

To the entire team at New Degree Press, thank you. Chelsea Friday! What can I say? As my marketing and revisions editor, you kept me moving forward and helped me calmly land this plane when I often felt anything but calm.

So many people gave me feedback on chapters of the book. I want to especially thank the following for taking the time to read large sections, providing thoughtful feedback, and allowing me to talk it out with you: Debra Williams, William Haynes, Blythe Keeler Robinson, Robert Daylin Brown, Derrick Weston Brown, Tedra Cheatham, James Williams, Raquiba LaBrie, and Noelle Cordeaux.

Last, but not least, I want to thank everyone who backed my book before there even was a book. Thank you so much for your support, for believing in me and my message.

Adam Butler	Audrey Jacobs
Adeola Whitney	Bernadine Battle
Aiko Bethea	Birgit Burton
Ajuah Helton	Blythe Keeler Robinson
Alicia Smith	Brandie Johnson
Allanah Rolph	Brett Jacobsen
Allegra Lawrence-Hardy	Callie Siegel
Andrea Ashmore	Carl Peoples
Andrea Fizer	Carmen Brown
Angie O'Neal	Carmen Mohan
Aquaria Smith	Carmen Randolph
Aubree Henderson	Cat H. Bradley

Catherine Finneran
Catherine Jefferson
Charisse M. Burns
Charmaine Walker
Che Watkins
Cheryl Crippen
Christine Barksdale
Christine Sperber
Cindy Ethridge
Conni Medina
Connie Cousins-Baker
Dan Israel
Dana Lupton
Danielle Davis
Danielle Kristine
Toussaint
David Gevertz
Debra Williams
Delroy Dennisur
Derrick Williams
Desirae Jones
Ed Patterson
Edel Howlin
Eldred Williams
Elika Aird
Elizabeth Zappa
Emily Christianson
Eric Koester
Erica Bullock-Jones
Geri Marvel
Gregory Morris
Hillary Dunson

James Ford
Jamie Novak
Jasán Ward
Jason Friedman
Jeffrey Ellman
Jenene Williams
Jessica Kohnen
Jessica Murphy
Johnny Rice II
Joi Jackson
Jomal W. Vailes
Joyce Butler
Julie Untener
Kanika Stanford
Kathryn Whitbourne
Kelli Doss
Kenmond Sanders
Kimberly Griffin Haynes
Kimberlyn Daniel
Kisha Solomon
Kristi Patterson
Kristin Jordan
Kristina Christy
Kweku Forstall
Laura Murvartian
Lenee Cook-Braxton
LeShante Wade
Levitica Watts
Lisa Bonner
Lisa Dwyer
Lisa Henry Horne
Lisa Noshay Petro

Lorenzo Jones
Lula Dawit
Lynn Avery Lewis
Maelle Fonteneau
Malesha Taylor
Marcus Cannady
Marina Paul
Marion H. Biglan
Marjorie Mitchell
Mary Benton
Mary Carole Cooper
Mary Nora Ford
Meagan Davies
Melanie White
Melissa George Bailey
Meredith McCreight
Michon Lartigue
Mike O'Brien
Monte Edwards
Morgan Wider
Nicole Momberg
Nimata Paul
Nzali Scales
Octavia Raheem
Oronike Odeleye
Paloma Garcia Lopez
Pam Covarrubias
Pam Davis
Pamel Faulkner
Patty Healy Janssen
Pi-Isis Ankhra
Primo Lasana

Qaadirah Abdur-Rahim
Raheem Beyah
Raquiba LaBrie
Rhonda Fischer
Richard Bakare
Robert Brown
Robin Sangston
Robin Simmons
Blackwell
Ronald Skeete
Ruby Morgan
Ruth Hamberg
Sanjay Parekh
Sara Fleming
Sara Moreno
Shameka Williams
Sharon A. Kendall
Sharon Calderon
Sharrod McClusky
Sherice Nicole
Shine-Cross
Simone Peart Boyce
Sonjui L. Kumar
Sonya Tinsley
Soukeyna Alexis
Stacey Key
Stephanie Dixon
Stephanie Mckay
Stephanie Zoccatelli
Susan Lee
Swami Jaya Devi
Tedra Cheatham

Theresa Flores
Theresa M. Robinson
Thomas Witherspoon
Three Merians
Tiffany Curtis
Tiffany D. Johnson
Tiffany Farmer
Tjuan Dogan
Tonika Dew Evans
Tracee Stanley
Tycely Williams

Vanya Francis
Vikram Kapoor
Vivian Carrasco
Wallace Sharif
Will Dawson
Wil Ozier
Yolanda Sanders
Yusef Sullivan
Yvonne Williams
Zenith Houston

APPENDIX

———

INTRODUCTION

Ackerman, Courtney E. "What Is Positive Psychology & Why Is It Important?" *PositivePsychology.com*, June 12, 2020. https://positivepsychology.com/what-is-positive-psychology-definition/.

Blue Zones. "Original Blue Zones Explorations." Accessed February 26, 2021. https://www.bluezones.com/live-longer-better/original-blue-zones/#section-1.

Coates, Ta-Nehisi. "The Case for Reparations." *The Atlantic*, June 2014. https://www.theatlantic.com/magazine/archive/2014/06/the-case-for-reparations/361631/.

Environmental Justice Organisations, Liabilities and Trade. "Needs." Accessed February 26, 2021. http://www.ejolt.org/2012/12/needs/.

Hersey, Tricia. "Rest–A Meticulous Love Practice with Tricia Hersey of The Nap Ministry." In *Radiant Rest Podcast with Tracee Stanley.* Produced by Baron Rinzler. Podcast, 24:03. https://www.radiantrest.com/episode-5-rest-a-meticulous-love-practice-with-tricia-hersey-of-the-nap-ministry/.

King, Danielle D., Ali, McCluney, and Bryant. "Give Black Employees Time to Rest and Recover." *Harvard Business Review,* February 22, 2021. https://hbr.org/2021/02/give-black-employees-time-to-rest-and-recover.

McCleod, Saul. "Maslow's Hierarchy of Needs." *Simple Psychology,* December 29, 2020. https://www.simplypsychology.org/maslow.html#gsc.tab=0.

Momodu, Samuel. "The Charleston Church Massacre (2015)." *BlackPast.org,* September 30, 2017. https://www.blackpast.org/african-american-history/charleston-church-massacre-2015/.

Rahman, Khaleda. "From George Floyd to Breonna Taylor, Remembering the Black People Killed by Police in 2020." *Newsweek,* December 29, 2020. https://www.newsweek.com/george-floyd-breonna-taylor-black-people-police-killed-1556285.

Weston Brown, Derrick. "We Can't Have Nothing." AJ+. July 15, 2020. YouTube video, 3:22.https://youtu.be/wFPBt5ZDA28.

CHAPTER 1

Botelho, Greg. "What Happened the Night Trayvon Martin Died." *CNN*, May 23, 2012. https://www.cnn.com/2012/05/18/justice/florida-teen-shooting-details.

Classic FM. "What are the lyrics and translation of 'O mio babbino caro'?" Accessed March 14, 2021. https://www.classicfm.com/composers/puccini/o-mio-babbino-caro-lyrics-translation/.

Georgetown University Library. "Sacred Arts of Orisha Traditions." Accessed February 28, 2021. https://www.library.georgetown.edu/exhibition/sacred-arts-orisha-traditions.

Mautz, Scott. "A 27-Year Study Says 1 Thing Is Key to Happiness and Longevity in Work and Life." *Inc.*, August 14, 2019. https://www.inc.com/scott-mautz/a-27-year-study-says-1-thing-is-key-to-happiness-longevity-in-work-life.html.

NAACP. "NAACP History: Lift Every Voice and Sing." Accessed January 14, 2021. https://www.naacp.org/naacp-history-lift-evry-voice-and-sing/.

The Gathering Spot. "Mission." Accessed January 14, 2021. https://thegatheringspot.club/why-we-gather-2/.

This Is Why We Gather. Atlanta: The Gathering Spot Holdings, LLC, 2020.

Wilson, Ryan. "As we close out Black History Month let's not forget that there isn't anything small or niche about Black people or Black culture." LinkedIn, February 27, 2021. https://www.linkedin.com/feed/update/urn:li:activity:6771450355642441728/

CHAPTER 2

Belt, Deb. "Atlanta Ranked No. 1 for Sex Trafficking; Conventions to Blame?" *Patch,* March 13, 2014. https://patch.com/georgia/buckhead/atlanta-ranked-no-1-for-sex-trafficking-conventions-to-blame.

Center on Juvenile and Criminal Justice. "Juvenile Justice History." Accessed January 29, 2021. http://www.cjcj.org/education1/juvenile-justice-history.html.

Cornell University. "History of Africana Studies at Cornell." Accessed January 29, 2021.https://africana.cornell.edu/node/1421.

Goodreads. "Audre Lorde > Quotes > Quotable Quote." Accessed January 29, 2021. https://www.goodreads.com/quotes/24893-i-have-come-to-believe-over-and-over-again-that.

Greig, Jon. "'Nobody's Free until Everybody's Free': Fannie Lou Hamer's Legacy Is More Important Now Than Ever." *Blavity,* October 07, 2019. https://blavity.com/blavity-original/nobodys-free-until-everybodys-free-fannie-lou-hamers-legacy-is-more-important-now-than-ever?category1=politics.

Jackson, Angelique and Jazz Tangcay. "Viola Davis and Stacey Abrams on Oscar Season, Politics and Wielding Their Power as Black Women." *Variety,* February 17, 2021. https://variety-com.cdn.ampproject.org/c/s/variety.com/2021/film/news/viola-davis-stacey-abrams-ma-raineys-black-bottom-all-in-1234908561/amp/.

Lowery, George. "A Campus Takeover That Symbolized an Era of Change." *Cornell Chronicle*, April 16, 2009. https://news.cornell. edu/stories/2009/04/campus-takeover-symbolized-era-change.

Ndlovu, Yvette Lisa. "Africana Center to Honor Founder at 50th Anniversary Symposium." *Cornell Chronicle*, April 9, 2019. https://news.cornell.edu/stories/2019/04/africana-cen-ter-honor-founder-50th-anniversary-symposium#:~:text=Co-rnell%20is%20considered%20the%20birthplace,African%20 ancestry%20throughout%20the%20world.

Odeleye, Oronike. "Oronike Odeleye Acceptance Speech— Inspi-ration Awards 2019." Breakthrough US. April 30, 2019. YouTube video, 1:41. https://www.youtube.com/watch?v=-ardCyPhsb4.

Sing, Bill. "Coca-Cola Acts to Cut All Ties with S. Africa." *Los Angeles Times,* September 18, 1986. https://www.latimes.com/ archives/la-xpm-1986-09-18-mn-11241-story.html

#MuteRKelly. "The #MuteRKelly Team." Accessed January 29, 2021. https://www.muterkelly.org/team?pgid=jgpfxqq4-48e1da-ab-2ff1-4414-ba4d-51b008532b04.

CHAPTER 3

American Psychological Association. "Mamie Phipps Clark, PhD, and Kenneth Clark, PhD." Accessed March 4, 2021. https:// www.apa.org/pi/oema/resources/ethnicity-health/psycholo-gists/clark.

Boseman, Chadwick. "Black Panther: Award Acceptance Speech 25th Annual SAG Awards." TNT. YouTube video, 3:28. https://www.youtube.com/watch?v=SgASaCn8XXs.

Disney. "A Film by Beyoncé Black Is King." Accessed March 4, 2021. https://disneyplusoriginals.disney.com/movie/black-is-king.

Fahamu Pecou Art. "The Official Website of Visual / Performing Artist & Scholar." Accessed March 4, 2021. https://www.fahamupecouart.com/.

Fahamu Pecou Art. "Trapademia III: 7 African Powers." Accessed March 3, 2021. https://www.fahamupecouart.com/artwork/trapademia-iii-seven-african-powers.

Flux Projects. "Remembrance as Resistance: Preserving Black Narratives." Accessed March 4, 2021. https://fluxprojects.org/productions/remembrance-as-resistance-preserving-black-narratives/.

High Museum of Art. "Imagining New Worlds: Wifredo Lam, José Parlá, Fahamu Pecou High Museum of Art." Accessed March 4, 2021. https://high.org/exhibition/imagining-new-worlds/.

Jackson, Angelique and Jazz Tangcay. "Viola Davis and Stacey Abrams on Oscar Season, Politics and Wielding Their Power as Black Women." *Variety,* February 17, 2021. https://variety-com.cdn.ampproject.org/c/s/variety.com/2021/film/news/viola-davis-stacey-abrams-ma-raineys-black-bottom-all-in-1234908561/amp/.

PBS. "The Murder of Emmett Till." Accessed March 4, 2021. https://www.pbs.org/wgbh/americanexperience/features/till-timeline/.

Pecou, Fahamu. "Emmett Still: A Short Film by Fahamu Pecou." YouTube video. https://www.youtube.com/watch?v=yok6KVI-OVOA&t=55s.

Pecou, Fahamu. "Regal Is as Regal Does..." *Art. Rap. Scholarshit*, August 04, 2020. https://scholarshit.tumblr.com/post/625543303885176832/regal-is-as-regal-does-2020-dr-fahamu.

Williams, Kimber. "Art for All: Fahamu Pecou Takes His Painting to the People." *Emory News Center*, June 30, 2016. https://news.emory.edu/stories/2016/06/er_fahamu_pecou_marta/campus.html.

CHAPTER 4

Footie Mob. "Mission Statement." Accessed January 29, 2021. https://footiemob.com/mission-statement/.

Mineo, Liz. "Good Genes Are Nice, but Joy Is Better." *The Harvard Gazette*, April 11, 2017. https://news.harvard.edu/gazette/story/2017/04/over-nearly-80-years-harvard-study-has-been-showing-how-to-live-a-healthy-and-happy-life/.

Murthy, Vivek H. *Together: The Healing Power of Human Connection in a Sometimes Lonely World*. New York: HarperCollins Publishers, 2020.

NBC Universal. "Tech Industry Fuels Reverse Migration for Black Americans (Part 2)." February 26, 2020. https://www.nbcnews.com/nightly-news/video/tech-industry-fuels-reverse-migration-for-black-americans-part-2-79472709895, :33.

Organ Historical Society. "Wicks Organ Co. (Opus 5874, 1982)." Accessed January 29, 2021. https://pipeorgandatabase.org/organ/37830.

CHAPTER 5

Anderson, Greta. "Police Fired for Injuring Spelman and Morehouse Students," *Inside Higher Ed*, June 3, 2020. https://www.insidehighered.com/quicktakes/2020/06/03/police-fired-injuring-spelman-and-morehouse-students.

Black Girl Magic: The Peloton Edition. "About." Facebook. https://www.facebook.com/groups/135928797220463.

Booker, Brakkton. "Former Atlanta Police Officer Who Shot Rayshard Brooks Charged with Felony Murder." *NPR*, June 17, 2020. https://www.npr.org/sections/live-updates-protests-for-racial-justice/2020/06/17/879509659/former-atlanta-police-officer-who-shot-rayshard-brooks-charged-with-felony-murde.

Cave Canem Foundation. "Mission and History." Accessed January 25, 2021. https://cavecanempoets.org/mission-history/.

Chatelain, Marcia. "What Mizzou Taught Me." *The Chronicle of Higher Education*, November 12, 2015. https://www.chronicle.com/article/what-mizzou-taught-me/.

Guobadia, Michelle. "Sometimes you crow and sometimes you fall." Facebook, January 17, 2021. https://www.facebook.com/groups/135928797220463/permalink/859352604878075.

Lowery, George. "A Campus Takeover That Symbolized an Era of Change." *Cornell Chronicle*, April 16, 2009. https://news.cornell.edu/stories/2009/04/campus-takeover-symbolized-era-change.

Young, Danielle. "6 Ava Duvernay Quotes to Reaffirm Your #Blackgirlmagic." *Essence,* July 2, 2016. https://www.essence.com/lifestyle/ava-duvernay-essence-empower-experience-speech/.

CHAPTER 6

Levenson, Eric, Amir Vera and Mallika Kallingal. "What We Know about the 5 Deaths in the Pro-trump Mob That Stormed the Capitol." *CNN*, January 8, 2021. https://www.cnn.com/2021/01/07/us/capitol-mob-deaths/index.html.

Palmer, Parker J. "The Gift of Presence, the Perils of Advice." *The On Being Project,* April 27, 2016. https://onbeing.org/blog/the-gift-of-presence-the-perils-of-advice/.

CHAPTER 7

Hurley, Katie. "What Is Resilience? Your Guide to Facing Life's Challenges, Adversities, and Crises." *Everyday Health*, December 10, 2020. https://www.everydayhealth.com/wellness/resilience/.

University of North Carolina Charlotte. "What is PTG?" Accessed February 1, 2021. https://ptgi.uncc.edu/what-is-ptg/.

CHAPTER 8

Ali, Shainna. "What Self-Love Isn't." *Psychology Today*, February 5th, 2019. https://www.psychologytoday.com/us/blog/modern-mentality/201902/what-self-love-isn-t.

Arie, India. "Worthy Q & A 1 of 2." June 4, 2018. In *Songversation*. Podcast, 7:30. https://anchor.fm/india-arie/episodes/Ep--2-SONGVERSATION-WORTHY-QA-1-of-2-e1j3ch.

Cadet, Danielle. "Your Black Colleagues May Look like They're Okay—Chances Are They're Not." *Refinery 29*, May 28, 2020. https://www.refinery29.com/en-us/2020/05/9841376/black-trauma-george-floyd-dear-white-people.

Ikpi, Bassey. *I'm Telling the Truth but I'm Lying*. New York: Harper Perennial, 2019.

Lizzo. "Self-Care Has to Be Rooted in Self-Preservation, Not Just Mimosas and Spa Days." *NBC Universal*, April 19, 2019. https://www.nbcnews.com/think/opinion/self-care-has-be-rooted-self-preservation-not-just-mimosas-ncna993661.

Mosley, Tonya and Allison Hagan. "'Mental Illness Is Not an Excuse, but It Is a Reason': How to Talk about Kanye West's Behavior." *WBUR*, June 29, 2020. https://www.wbur.org/here-andnow/2020/07/29/kanye-west-mental-health.

CHAPTER 9

A&E Television Networks. "Eric Garner Dies in NYPD Chokehold." Accessed February 6, 2021. https://www.history.com/this-day-in-history/eric-garner-dies-nypd-chokehold.

American Psychological Association. "More Sleep Would Make Most Americans Happier, Healthier and Safer." Accessed February 6, 2021. https://www.apa.org/research/action/sleep-deprivation.

DeSilver, Drew. "As Coronavirus Spreads, Which U.S. Workers Have Paid Sick Leave–and Which Don't?" *Pew Research Center,* March 12, 2020. https://www.pewresearch.org/fact-tank/2020/03/12/as-coronavirus-spreads-which-u-s-workers-have-paid-sick-leave-and-which-dont/.

Hersey, Tricia. "Rest–A Meticulous Love Practice with Tricia Hersey of The Nap Ministry." In *Radiant Rest Podcast with Tracee Stanley.* Produced by Baron Rinzler. Podcast, 24:03. https://www.radiantrest.com/episode-5-rest-a-meticulous-love-practice-with-tricia-hersey-of-the-nap-ministry/.

McCarty Carino, Meghan. "American Workers Can Suffer Vacation Guilt … If They Take Vacations at All." *Marketplace,* July 12, 2019. https://www.marketplace.org/2019/07/12/american-workers-vacation-guilt/.

Merriam-Webster, Incorporated. "Inspiration." Accessed March 11, 2021. https://www.merriam-webster.com/dictionary/inspiration?utm_campaign=sd&utm_medium=serp&utm_source=jsonld.

Merriam-Webster, Incorporated. "Sabbath." Accessed February 6, 2021. https://www.merriam-webster.com/dictionary/Sabbath.

Raheem, Octavia. *Gather.* Octavia F. Raheem, 2020.

Resnick, Brian. "The Racial Inequality of Sleep." *Atlantic*, October 27, 2015. https://www.theatlantic.com/health/archive/2015/10/the-sleep-gap-and-racial-inequality/412405/.

Stanley, Tracee. *Radiant Rest: Yoga Nidra for Deep Relaxation and Awakened Clarity*. Boulder: Shambhala, 2021.

The Nap Ministry. "Our Work Has a Framework." Accessed February 6, 2021. https://thenapministry.wordpress.com/.

The Nap Ministry (@thenapministry). "A Care and Justice Strategy." Instagram photo, September 30, 2020. https://www.instagram.com/p/CFxJFgqFRYp/.

CHAPTER 10

Black Joy Archive. Accessed March 11, 2021. https://www.black-joyarchive.com/.

Black Joy Parade. "Mission." Accessed March 11, 2021. https://www.blackjoyparade.org/about.

Jacob's Pillow Dance Festival. "Dance of the African Diaspora Pearl Primus." Accessed March 11, 2021. https://dancein-teractive.jacobspillow.org/themes-essays/african-diaspora/pearl-primus/.

Ward, Jasán. "LIFE: Love. Intention. Focus. Empowerment." Facebook, June 28, 2019. https://www.facebook.com/groups/877061746012996.

CHAPTER 11

Akil, Bakari. "The Power of Positive Immersion–Is Your Environment Right for You?" *Psychology Today,* February 4, 2010. https://www.psychologytoday.com/us/blog/communication-central/201002/the-power-positive-immersion-is-your-environment-right-you.

Boseman, Chadwick. "Chadwick Boseman's Howard University 2018 Commencement Speech." Howard University, May 12, 2018. YouTube video, 31:46. https://www.youtube.com/watch?v-=RIHZypMyQ2s.

Gambino, Lauren. "'I won't be the last': Kamala Harris, first woman elected US vice-president, accepts place in history," *The Guardian,* November 8, 2020. https://www.theguardian.com/us-news/2020/nov/07/kamala-harris-victory-speech-first-woman-vice-president.

JRNI. "Our Mission Is Simple Helping Adventurous Life Coaches Launch Thriving Practices." Accessed March 12, 2021.https://www.jrni.co/about#instructors.

Made in the USA
Las Vegas, NV
19 October 2021